WITHDRAWN

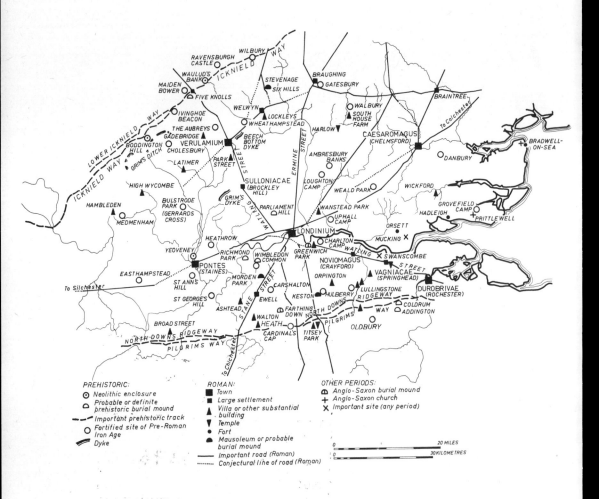

PREHISTORIC:
⊙ Neolithic enclosure
⌒ Probable or definite prehistoric burial mound
– – – Important prehistoric track
○ Fortified site of Pre-Roman Iron Age
〰 Dyke

ROMAN:
■ Town
■ Large settlement
▲ Villa or other substantial building
● Temple
● Fort
◖ Mausoleum or probable burial mound
—— Important road (Roman)
······ Conjectural line of road (Roman)

OTHER PERIODS:
⊞ Anglo-Saxon burial mound
✝ Anglo-Saxon church
✕ Important site (any period)

Frontispiece   The London Region

REGIONAL ARCHAEOLOGIES

The Archaeology of London

BY RALPH MERRIFIELD

HEINEMANN EDUCATIONAL BOOKS   LONDON

Regional Archaeologies

GENERAL EDITOR: D. M. Wilson, M.A., F.S.A.
Professor of Medieval Archaeology
in the University of London

Heinemann Educational Books Ltd
LONDON EDINBURGH MELBOURNE TORONTO
AUCKLAND SINGAPORE JOHANNESBURG
HONG KONG NAIROBI IBADAN NEW DELHI

For Jenny and Michael

ISBN 0 435 32967 7

Published by Heinemann Educational Books Ltd
48 Charles Street, London W1X 8AH
Printed in Great Britain
by Fletcher and Son Ltd, Norwich

Contents

List of Illustrations

Acknowledgements

The author gratefully acknowledges all the help he has received in discussion of the problems of London archaeology with his colleagues of the Guildhall and London Museums, and especially with Miss Jean Macdonald concerning the prehistory of the region. He is also very grateful to Professor W. F. Grimes, Professor D. M. Wilson and Mr John Wymer for making helpful suggestions and corrections in the sections which they kindly read. Any errors that may remain, or that have crept in during later revisions, are the author's sole responsibility.

He is particularly grateful to Mrs D. M. Wilson both for her excellent line-drawings and for her good advice in all matters relating to the illustrations. Photographs have been kindly supplied by Mrs M.U. Jones (*fig. 40*), Lt. Col. G.W. Meates (*fig. 38*), the British Museum (*figs. 2, 29, 30a, 31*), Guildhall Museum (*figs. 34, 39, 41*), London Museum (*figs. 8, 9, 14, 15, 17, 23*), Verulamium Museum (*figs. 32, 35*), and Aerofilms Ltd. (*fig. 24*). The author is also much indebted to Mr R. Robertson Mackay for kindly supplying a revised plan of Staines Causewayed Camp. Other plans and sections have been derived by kind permission of the following sources: *The Journal of the Royal Anthropological Institute* (*fig. 4*), Professor W.F. Grimes (*fig. 22*), Sir Mortimer Wheeler (*figs. 26 and 27*), Guildhall Museum (*fig. 33*). Thanks are due to the British Museum and the London Museum for permission to photograph coins in their collections, and to the Vicar of All Hallows Barking Church for permission to photograph the Anglo-Saxon arch there.

Dating

The study of prehistory has been revolutionized in recent years by the development of new scientific methods of dating. The most important of these is radio-carbon dating. It is known that when any organism, animal or vegetable, dies, it contains radio-active carbon (called Carbon 14) absorbed from the atmosphere. This gradually decays and loses its radio-activity at a regular rate. By measuring this radio-activity, it is therefore possible to estimate age, within a certain margin of error.

Recently the results obtained from radio-carbon dating have been checked by another method of dating—tree-ring analysis (dendrochronology), which is based on the fact that a tree adds one ring of growth each year, varying in width according to the wetness of the growing season. Some trees—especially the Californian Bristle Cone Pine—live for several thousand years, so it is possible, by over-lapping tree-ring patterns obtained from a number of trees, modern and ancient, to give an exact date to wood that is thousands of years old. The comparison of the date obtained in this way with that from radio-carbon dating, has shown there is a considerable error in the latter for certain periods. Radio-carbon, in fact, seems to have given a date that is consistently too recent in the period covered by our later prehistory—as the Egyptologists have always maintained, since radio-carbon dating of early Dynastic objects was more recent than the date that could be worked out historically for Egypt.

The apparent need to re-set the hands of the radio-carbon 'clock' has been taken into account in this book, so that dates in later prehistory are somewhat earlier than those accepted in recent years—and much earlier than those generally accepted fifteen years ago. It is likely that further revisions will be required.

The dating of the Palaeolithic period is an approximation taken from estimates made by various methods—astronomical, geological and radio-active. The most promising is based on the regular decay of radio-active Potassium (Potassium-Argon dating), but its application to Palaeolithic archaeology is still in its infancy.

1 The London Region

The London region today is dominated by the sprawling mass that is Greater London, an area of more than 600 square miles that is mainly covered by streets and buildings, and occupied by nearly 8,000,000 people. Beyond, and intermeshed with the 'Drives' and 'Avenues' of the outer suburbs, open country survives for a few miles before the ring of satellite towns is reached. Some of these are historic towns in their own right, others new towns built to receive the overflow from London's population, all of them linked by busy highways and adding to the urbanization of the region. It is not easy to imagine all this swept away, and the countryside as it would have been in prehistoric and early historic times. Even the surviving countryside has been much altered by later farming and quarrying, and there are very few places where we have a glimpse of its natural condition. The River Thames still divides the region into two parts, although it is less of a barrier than in the days when it had only one bridge or none at all. It is still a water highway of some importance, but no longer provides the only means of easy travel as it did in the past.

The region is bounded on the north-west by a ridge of chalk, the Chiltern Hills, running from south-west to north-east, and divided from the Berkshire Downs and the chalk uplands of Wessex to the south-west only by the narrow valley of the Middle Thames at the Goring Gap above Reading.

The southern boundary is another chalk ridge, the North Downs of Kent and Surrey, running from east to west and continuing westward into Hampshire to join the Wessex uplands.

Between these chalk ridges lies the wedge-shaped London Basin, where the layer of chalk, formed on a sea-bed about 100 million years ago, dips in a trough beneath a more recent formation, the London Clay, which was formed beneath a tropical sea between 40 and 70 million years ago. It contains, in addition to shells and other fossils of sea creatures, the seeds of palm-trees and the remains of crocodiles, showing that land was near, and suggesting that the London Clay was formed in the estuary of a river. This was long before men existed, but the age of the giant reptiles was over, and there were many kinds of warm-blooded animals, the majority very different from those of today.

The London Clay lies immediately beneath the top-soil over much of the London Basin, bluish-grey in the depths, but yellowish-brown near the surface. Since water cannot pass through it, the ground above often becomes water-logged in wet weather. In its natural condition it is heavily wooded with oak trees and a thick undergrowth of hazel or hornbeam.

ANCIENT RIVER GRAVELS

Fortunately, in many places in the Thames Valley the London Clay is overlaid by later deposits of gravel and sand that are more favourable for human occupation. These were laid down by the river and its tributaries in the last 1¾ million years, during the most recent (Pleistocene) geological period. This included the Great Ice Age when part of Britain was covered at least four times by an ice-sheet. At its greatest extent, about 400,000 years ago, this reached as far south as North London. Each of these cold phases lasted for many thousands of years, although the climate did not remain equally severe throughout. The glacial periods were divided by periods called interglacials, when the climate became very much warmer, so that forests could grow.

Fig. 1 The formation of gravel terraces

A, C and E: warm phases with high sea level; B and D: glacial phases with low sea level

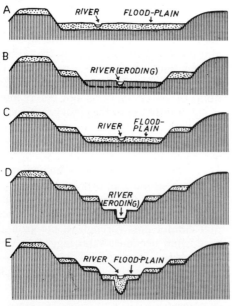

These changes of climate caused great variation in the sea level. Vast quantities of seawater were locked up in ice-sheets during the glacial periods, and were then released through melting in the warmer

periods that followed. The great pressure of the ice-sheets on the land they covered, and the removal of this compression when the ice disappeared also probably had some effect. When the sea level was high, the Thames flowed slowly in a winding course and was regularly flooded; when the sea level dropped, the river flowed swiftly and cut itself a deep channel, leaving its old bed as a terrace at a higher level. We therefore find ancient river gravels at various heights in the Thames Valley. Since, in spite of the occasions when the process was temporarily reversed, the general tendency over the last million and a half years has been for the sea-level to drop in relation to the land, the earlier gravels are generally the higher; although there was one period in the last glaciation when the sea was so low that the Thames cut itself a bed, called the Buried Channel, 100ft below its present level. (*See fig. 1*). There is an upper gravel terrace at about 100 to 120 ft above present sea-level, called the Boyn Hill Terrace (after a site in Maidenhead); a middle gravel terrace at about 50 ft above sea level, called the Taplow Terrace (after a site on the opposite side of the river in Buckinghamshire); and a lower terrace at about 10-15 ft above sea level, called the Flood Plain Terrace, which forms the present banks of the Thames and the floor of its valley. In many places it is eroded and overlaid by more recent river-silt, which has formed marshes beside the river. Even the higher terraces do not provide a dry gravel subsoil everywhere, since their uppermost layer, where it survives, is often a clay-like loam called brick-earth, most generally found on the Taplow Terrace. It is wooded under natural conditions, whereas a surface of the drier gravels and sands is less over-grown. This could be occupied by prehistoric men without laborious clearance, and the light soils could be cultivated by the most primitive methods. Another great advantage was a ready supply of water, both from tributaries of the Thames and from the springs which poured from the slope of the terrace where the gravel overlay the impermeable London Clay. These underground waters were later exploited more conveniently by sinking shallow wells to the base of the gravel.

2 Hunters of the Old Stone Age

In the ancient gravels of the Thames are found the bones and teeth of the animals that lived in the valley when the river flowed in these higher beds. Some are animals especially adapted for a cold climate, like the Mammoth (a woolly elephant), the Woolly Rhinoceros and the Musk Ox; others are warmth-loving animals, like the Straight-Tusked Elephant and the Hippopotamus. These finds indicate the great contrast of climate between the cold periods and the warm interglacials; but in some deposits both types of elephant, for example, have been found together, and therefore presumably lived in the transitional climate at the beginning or end of an interglacial. There is abundant evidence that ancient men lived in the Thames Valley at the same time as these long extinct animals. Although as yet the actual human remains of only one individual have been found, the chipped flint tools and weapons of these Palaeolithic (Old Stone Age) people are common in the river gravels and brick-earths.

London is credited with the first recorded find of a Palaeolithic tool associated with an extinct animal, although its significance was not understood at the time. About 1690, John Conyers, an apothecary interested in antiquities, was digging for gravel 'in a field near to the Sign of Sir John Oldcastle in the Fields, not far from Battlebridge and near to the river of Wells', according to his friend Bagford, who wrote an account of the find in 1715 (published in Hearne's edition of Leland's *Collectanea*). The site has been identified in the King's Cross Road near Granville Square, 200 yards east of Gray's Inn Road, and lies on the Middle (Taplow) Terrace. Here Conyers found 'the body of an Elephant', evidently the bones of a mammoth, easily reconizable as an elephant by its teeth and tusks. He also found 'a Flint Lance like unto the Head of a Spear', which is now in the British Museum (*fig. 2*). The early 18th century antiquaries who pondered the problem 'How this Elephant came there' naturally remembered the one occasion recorded in early history when elephants were brought to Britain, and concluded

```
0   1   2   3   4   5   6   7   8   9   10  cm

0           1           2           3           4  in.
```

Fig. 2 Acheulian flint hand-axe from King's Cross Road, found about 1690 with elephant bones

that it came to Britain with the Emperor Claudius, who was accompanied by a corps of elephants in the Roman invasion of A.D. 43. The pointed flint was of course explained as a weapon used by an ancient Briton against the elephant. It is easy to laugh at these early antiquaries, but it must be remembered that this was a period when it was generally believed that the world was created only 6000 years ago, and the idea that these relics could be more than 100,000 years old would have been unimaginable. Two correct identifications were made, however; the animal remains were recognized as those of an elephant, improbable as it must have seemed, and the pointed flint was recognized as a weapon of human workmanship. Moreover, the deduction was made that these objects from the same gravel bed were ancient and contemporary with each other—not necessarily quite correct, since the chipped flint may have been washed out of an earlier gravel, but foreshadowing the arguments of all later archaeologists.

It was in fact no less a person than Colonel Lane-Fox, later to become famous as the formidable General Pitt-Rivers, father of scientific archaeology, who first proved by similar discoveries of humanly worked flints associated with mammoth remains in the gravel of the Taplow Terrace near Churchfield Road, Acton, that there were men in the Thames Valley as early as the period of these extinct animals. Lane-Fox's observations, however, were

4

made between 1869 and 1872, when new ideas about the antiquity of man, based on similar finds in the river gravels of the Somme some years earlier, were at last being accepted; although opposition to them was by no means dead, and as recently as 1863 a French geologist in a high official position had suggested that the chipped flints from the Somme might be of Roman origin.

HAND-AXES

The implements that had first attracted attention in France, as in England, were chipped to an oval or pear shape, with a sharp edge all round, except sometimes at the wider end. This was often thicker, and in some cases was left unchipped, showing the original outer surface of the flint. It seemed clear, therefore, that the wider part was held in the hand, and this type of implement came to be called a hand-axe. It must have served many purposes, and would have been an effective weapon. Its commonest use was probably for skinning and cutting up animals, but it could also have been used for stripping the bark from trees, splitting wood and bones, and even for digging. Those with a cutting edge all round could have been thrown as dangerous missiles, or may even have been hafted in some way, possibly by binding a withy round the middle, like the stone tomahawks of the Australian Aborigines. One thing is reasonably certain, however; the hand-axe was not hafted like a spear-head to a long shaft, as its superficial appearance might suggest, and as the 18th century antiquaries thought. The thickness of the butt and the weight of most hand-axes would make such a use quite impracticable, and Bagford's story that the Gray's Inn Road implement was found 'fastened into a Shaft of a good length' is unlikely to be true. The only indication of possible hafting that may be authentic was a discovery at Bedford of what appeared to be stems of rushes, wrapped round the butt-end of a hand-axe when it was first exposed. These, however, were probably merely a protection for the hand, as the finder himself believed, and there is no reason to doubt that most hand-axes were used in the way that their name implies. The usefulness of this general-purpose tool and weapon is shown by its continued manufacture over an immensely long period, extending in the Thames Valley at least through two Interglacials. In Africa, where it was probably first developed, it must have an even longer history, which began in a still more remote period.

THE EARLIEST STONE TOOLS

The hand-axe, however, is a highly evolved tool, consisting as it does of the carefully shaped core of a flint nodule or pebble, from which the entire surface, or the greater part of the surface, has been removed by chipping. This is by no means an obvious thing to do with a piece of stone in order to make it into a cutting tool, and the task could only be performed by an expert who was thoroughly familiar with his material. Such skill was gradually acquired through many generations of flint-chipping, and the hand-axe itself was slowly evolved from more primitive chopping tools, in which an edge was produced by knocking off chips or flakes first from one side and then from the other, so that the scar or facet left by one flake was used as the striking surface to remove the next. The flakes themselves were equally useful for cutting and scraping. Primitive chopper-core industries are known to be of immense antiquity in East and South Africa, where they date from the beginning of the

Pleistocene period, perhaps 1,750,000 years ago, and are associated with ape-like men of the kind called *Homo habilis*. Industries of this kind continued with little change for a very long period of time, and are widely distributed in Africa, Asia and Central Europe. In China and south-east Asia they are of Middle Pleistocene date, and are associated with the more highly developed ape-like men called *Peking* and *Java Man*—now considered to be truly human and of the same zoological family as ourselves. They walked upright, and have therefore been named *Homo* (formerly *Pithecanthropus*) *erectus*.

THE CLACTONIAN INDUSTRY

A crude flint industry of the chopper-core type was introduced into what is now south-east Britain near the beginning of the *Hoxnian* Interglacial, some 300,000 years ago, or just possibly in the less cold (interstadial) phase of the preceding (*Lowestoft*) Glaciation. This is the first evidence of human beings in Britain. The industry is called *Clactonian*, since it was first recognized at Clacton-on-Sea, and its characteristic tools are rough choppers produced by alternate flaking as already described, and large flakes, sometimes trimmed by secondary chipping along the edge for use as scrapers or borers, but often, no doubt, used without further work as knives (*fig. 3*). A flake deliberately produced by man always has a flat top or striking platform on which the blow fell to detach it; a plain, unfacetted back that fitted against the parent nodule; and a distinct bulb or swelling, called the bulb of percussion, on the back just below the point of impact. The striking platform of a typical Clactonian flake makes a wide angle with the back, where the bulb of percussion is prominent. It has been found by experiment that flakes of this kind can be

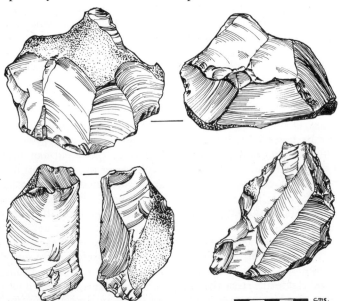

Fig. 3 Clactonian flint core and flake tools from Lower Gravel of 100 ft terrace at Swanscombe

6

produced by swinging blows with a hard hammerstone, such as a heavy quartzite pebble, or by bashing the nodule to be chipped against a large flint used as an anvil. It is often impossible to tell whether a flint core was intended for use as a tool, or was simply a waste product in the manufacture of flakes. The broken point of a wooden spear and several bones used as tools were also found at Clacton, showing that Clactonian man did not rely only on stone. The surviving tools of all Stone Age

Acheulian, after the type site of St Acheul, near Amiens.

THE ACHEULIAN INDUSTRY

The more developed forms of Acheulian hand-axes have already been described, since these beautiful implements from the ancient river gravels were the first to attract the notice of modern man. There are, however, many cruder examples, roughly chipped with a hammerstone like the Clactonian chopper-cores. Many of these

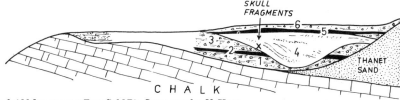

Fig. 4 Section through 100 ft terrace at Barnfield Pit, Swanscombe, N. Kent

people must give us a very incomplete picture of their culture.

The Clactonians lived and hunted in the Lower Thames Valley, and their characteristic flint industry without hand-axes has been found at Little Thurrock, Essex, and on the opposite side of the river at Swanscombe, Kent. Flint-chipping in the Clactonian style has also been found farther up the river and near Reading, but here it is associated with hand-axes, and may be a later survival. The clearest evidence for the early date of the pure Clactonian comes from the gravel terrace 100 ft above sea-level at Swanscombe. Here, in the Barnfield Gravel Pit, the sections showed a lower, middle, and upper bed of gravel, separated by layers of loam (*fig. 4*). In the Lower Gravel and overlying loam (1 and 2) were found the crude flakes and cores of the Clactonian, associated with bones of the straight-tusked elephant, rhinoceros and horse. Above, in the Middle Gravel (3 and 4), were found many hand-axes, typical of the industry called

are rough-outs for hand-axes of the better type, abandoned before they were finished. Others—and there were great numbers of these at Swanscombe—are small tools hastily made and presumably for temporary use. Both kinds are associated, at Swanscombe and elsewhere, with hand-axes of the more developed types. The rougher hand-axes alone, however, have been found in an ancient bed of the Thames 150 ft above the present river level between Reading and Henley. These may possibly represent an early stage of the Acheulian.

The better implements of the Middle Acheulian have been finally shaped by the delicate removal of thin flakes. Experiment has shown that this can best be done with a long cylindrical piece of wood, bone or antler, used as a hammer. Some fine hand-axes are pointed, occasionally with incurved sides; others are oval or ovate; and many are chipped so that the edge of the side, seen in profile, makes an elegant curve like a reversed *S* (*fig. 5*). The shapeliness of these tools must have given great pleasure

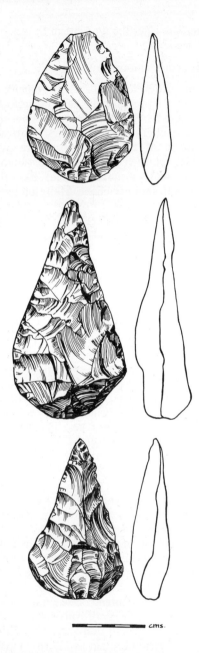

to their makers and owners, and even modern man, without exact knowledge of the way in which they were used, cannot help feeling satisfaction in handling them.

SWANSCOMBE MAN

What did these mysterious Acheulians look like? Swanscombe again has provided part of the answer. In 1935, 1936 and 1955, fragments of a human skull were found in the Middle Gravel of the Barnfield Pit—the most important Palaeolithic discovery in Britain, for Acheulian hand-axes were found in close association with them. The skull is not unlike that of modern man, and the brain is only slightly smaller. Unfortunately the front of the skull is missing, so that nothing is known of the face, but a similar skull from Steinheim in Germany had the strong brow ridges that usually accompany heavy projecting jaws. These, however, would have been less massive and ape-like than the earlier jawbone from Mauer, near Heidelberg, which belonged to a man of the *Homo erectus* type. It seems likely that the Clactonian industry had been introduced by men of this more primitive kind.

THE LEVALLOISIAN INDUSTRY

The typical Acheulian hand-axe was a core tool, but chips and flakes were also used, sometimes with secondary working, as they were in the Clactonian. As yet, these were irregular in shape and could not be produced to a required size or pattern; but towards the end of the warm period (the Hoxnian Interglacial) during which Swanscombe Man and the Acheulian culture had flourished, a new technique for making flakes appeared. This was by first chipping a prepared core with one face fairly flat, called from its shape a 'tortoise core'. From this a large flake could be struck, so that part of the flat face formed one side. Since it

Fig. 5 Middle Acheulian flint hand axes from Swanscombe

8

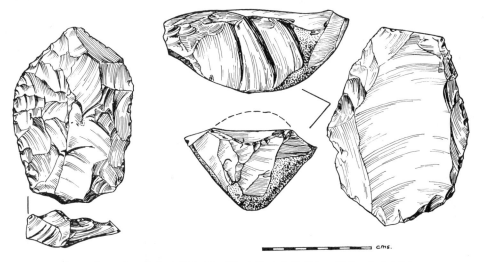

Fig. 6 Levallois flint industry from Baker's Hole, Northfleet, Kent. Left, flake with facetted striking platform (below); right 'tortoise' core with flake scar

was struck from a chipped core, a flake of this kind usually has facetting on the top or striking platform *(fig. 6)*. A large broad flake of this type, with a little secondary working could be made into a tool like a hand-axe, while a long narrow flake could be used as a knife. This technique is called *Levalloisian,* after its type site of Levallois-Perret, near Paris.

Levalloisian industries continued in the Thames Valley during the milder phases of the succeeding Glaciation (*Gipping*), and a working-floor of a temperate period was found at Baker's Hole, Northfleet. The 'Levalloisian also continued through the Interglacial that followed (called the *Ipswichian*). At West Drayton an industry similar to that at Baker's Hole was found, but at Crayford and Acton, which probably represent a later phase, long narrow blades predominated. These were struck from a 'prismatic core', prepared by striking parallel flakes from one or both ends. In a brick-earth pit near Crayford a surface was found where flints had been chipped, and it

was possible to reconstruct a flint nodule by replacing all the flakes in position. These knife-blades had evidently been made to cut up animals, whose bones were found there, and one flake actually lay on the jawbone of a woolly rhinoceros. What the hunters themselves were like we do not know, but on the Continent, during the last Interglacial and later, another, possibly related, flake industry (the *Mousterian*) was associated with Neandertal Man, a being with a relatively large brain, but with strongly projecting brow ridges and jaw. It seems likely that the people who produced the Levalloisian flake tools were of similar general type, possibly descended from the more primitive Neandertaloids like Swanscombe Man, who may also be near the direct line of descent of modern man.

OCCUPATION OF THE THAMES VALLEY

Levalloisians may have survived in the Thames Valley during the earlier part of the last Glaciation (called *Weichselian*),

9

but on our present evidence the region seems then to have been deserted for many thousands of years, even during a comparatively mild phase. In south-west France Neandertal men were replaced by men of the modern type, who were artists as well as hunters, and drew on the walls of caves fine pictures of the animals they pursued. As far as we know, none of these Advanced Palaeolithic people entered the Thames Valley, although game was to be found there and Britain was still linked to the Continent by a land-bridge. The ice-sheet itself lay much farther north, and the only reason for the apparent absence of human life for so long seems to be the lack of convenient shelter in a rockless region.

It was now the turn of the Dordogne and similar areas to support a flourishing hunting population, but the Thames Valley itself, with its abundance of flint, had been equally favoured at a much earlier period by the Acheulian hand-axe makers of the Second (Hoxnian) Interglacial. Judging

10,000 years ago	WEICHSELIAN GLACIATION	Buried Channel of Thames (over 100 ft below sea level) Sands and gravels of Flood Plain
70,000 years ago	IPSWICHIAN INTERGLACIAL	Brick earth on gravel between Iver and Acton and at Crayford
100,000 years ago	GIPPING GLACIATION	Taplow Terrace at about 50 ft Brick-earths and gravels at 80 to 100 ft Boyn Hill gravel terrace (may belong to preceding interglacial)
200,000 years ago	HOXNIAN INTERGLACIAL	100 ft gravel terrace at Swanscombe
300,000 years ago	LOWESTOFT GLACIATION	boulder clays brought by ice-sheet to Finchley and St Albans, diverting the Thames
400,000 years ago		

Fig. 7 Time chart of the Old Stone Age

10

from the enormous number of these tools found in its gravels, it must then have been a happy hunting-ground of woodlands teeming with wild life, and supporting a human population that was very small by the standards of more recent settled farming communities, but probably exceptionally large for a primitive people dependent for its food on what could be hunted or found growing wild.

It is difficult to offer a clear chronological sequence in which human cultures, climatic phases and geological features are related to one another, for geologists are not yet in agreement about the dating of the gravel terraces, and there is the added complication that stone tools found in them may have been washed out of a much earlier deposit. The table given below is therefore provisional, and the dates given are so approximate that they really only give a general idea of the sort of time-span involved. This is so vast that it cannot easily be comprehended.

Poplar Willow Juniper Grasses and sedges	Irish Deer Reindeer Horse Woolly Mammoth Woolly Rhinoceros	Thames Valley deserted (?) continuation of Levalloisian
Birch Hazel Oak Alder	Woolly Mammoth Straight-Tusked Elephant Rhinoceros Hippopotamus Red Deer Bison Cave Lion	Levalloisian (Ebbsfleet, Crayford, Acton and Iver) Late Acheulian (?) Stoke Newington
Grasses and sedges	Woolly Mammoth Woolly Rhinoceros Wolf Horse Cave Lion Reindeer Arctic Fox	Levalloisian (Northfleet, West Drayton) Specialized hand-axe types of the Late Middle Acheulian Some use of Levallois technique
Pinewoods Hazel Alder Yew	Straight-Tusked Elephant Rhinoceros Horse Deer Cave Lion Cave Bear	Beginnings of Levallois technique Middle Acheulian (Swanscombe Man) Clactonian
grasses and sedges beyond edge of ice-sheet		Possibly Early (?) Acheulian and Clactonian in warmer phase

3 Hunters and Fishermen of the Middle Stone Age

AFTER THE ICE AGE

The melting of the last great ice-sheet about 10,000 years ago marks the end of the Pleistocene geological epoch, and the beginning of the present epoch (called the *Holocene*). As the weather grew milder, trees, first birch and later pine, gradually spread over north-western Europe, and forests replaced the open grasslands and mossy tundra of the glacial period. With these also disappeared the great animals that had roamed them—the mammoth, woolly rhinoceros, bison and reindeer; their place being taken by the animals of the forest—the red deer, roe deer, wild ox and pig. There followed a period of warm dry summers and cold winters, called the *Boreal* phase. The sea-level was lower than at the present day, and south-eastern England was still joined to the Continent. What is now the North Sea was a marshy plain, with pine-woods in its higher places, such as the Dogger Bank; and it could easily be crossed with the aid of light canoes. Such were the conditions between about 8000 and 6000 B.C. Then a general sinking of the land began, and all this low-lying land was submerged, so that Britain became separated from the Continent by sea. A milder and wetter climate was induced, in which deciduous trees such as the oak, lime, elm and alder flourished, gradually replacing the pines and birches. This period, called the *Atlantic* phase, continued until about 3000 B.C. Botanists have studied the changing proportions of tree species resulting from these climatic changes, and useful evidence for the dating of peat beds in the period after the Ice Age can be obtained by comparing the numbers of pollen grains of the various species in a sample of the peat.

THE MAGLEMOSEANS

In the Baltic area, descendants of the latest Palaeolithic people of eastern Europe had successfully adapted their way of life to the new conditions. To the knife-blades and other narrow flake implements of their ancestors they had added an important new tool, that was of the greatest value to forest-dwellers. This was the hafted axe, a purposefully shaped flint core like the Lower Palaeolithic hand-axe, but with the broader end given a sharp cutting edge by striking off a flake from the side (cf. *figs. 8 and 10b*). This is called in French a *tranchet,* and tools of this kind are called *tranchet-axes.* They were hafted as axes or adzes by wedging the butt into a socket made in a stout piece of red-deer antler, which was holed to take a wooden handle. When the edge became blunt, the axe could be resharpened by the removal of another flake across the cutting end. A new weapon was the stone mace-head, made by pecking a hollow on each side of a pebble until there was an hour-glass shaped hole through the middle, presumably used for hafting as a stone-headed club. Bows were used with arrows tipped or barbed with tiny flint points of various shapes, called *microliths*, or with heads that had a cutting edge instead of a point, probably for shooting birds and small game. As important as stone tools and weapons, however, were those made of bone and antler. Slender barbed spear-points were carved in bone with a graver, a flint which had a narrow chisel-shaped edge. Pieces of red-deer antler were made into adze- or axe-like tools by grinding to an edge, and were probably used for grubbing up edible roots or excavating hollows for shelter.

These Mesolithic (Middle Stone Age) people of the North European plain were fishermen as well as hunters, and preferred to settle on the banks of rivers and lakes, in places that were often marshy. They are named *Maglemoseans* after a site in Denmark—the words *magle mose* mean 'big bog'. They were equipped with boats (either dug-out canoes, or lighter craft made of skins or bark on a wooden frame) and had no difficulty in crossing the fens and narrow water-courses of what is now the North Sea, but was then merely a continuation of their familiar North European plain. The banks of the Thames and its tributaries provided the sort of home to which they were accustomed, with abundant fish, fowl and small game in the river, fens and forest, and with gravel ridges that were suitable for camping. Until some evidence is found for the presence of Advanced Palaeolithic men, like those who appeared in France during the last glacial period, these Maglemoseans of the early Boreal phase of climate, 8000-9000 years ago, must be regarded as the earliest men of the modern type (*Homo sapiens*) to inhabit the London region.

MAGLEMOSEANS OF THE THAMES VALLEY

At Broxbourne in the Upper Lea Valley, the small camping site of a family group of this period was found on a ridge of sand overlying the gravel of the flood plain. It was covered by peat, which could be dated to the Boreal period of about 6000 B.C. by an analysis of the pollen that it contained. The flint tools included gravers used for working bone and antler, all traces of which had unfortunately decayed and vanished. They also included scrapers for cleaning skins for use as clothing, and perhaps also for making tents. The relationship of these people with the Maglemoseans of the Baltic region was shown by the presence of the typical tranchet axes, with the flakes struck in sharpening them. There were also examples of the little flint microliths, made by first notching and then snapping a narrow flake to produce a triangular arrowhead or barb. This technique had been adopted by the western Maglemoseans from their neighbours to the south, who had a more elaborate microlithic industry of African origin, in which tiny implements were produced in a number of geometric forms.

Associated groups of stone tools and other worked flints like those at Broxbourne were found similarly stratified under peat and over gravel near the Hackney Brook, a feeder of the Lea (now buried), and in the valley of the Colne near Uxbridge and Harefield. On a site recorded in 1890 in Spring Gardens, St James's Park, flint implements, including scrapers, were found on an old post-glacial land surface near a channel of the Tyburn. Overlying them was a bed containing a fragment of the shell of a tortoise, of a kind that could have lived here only when the climate was warmer than it is today. This must have

13

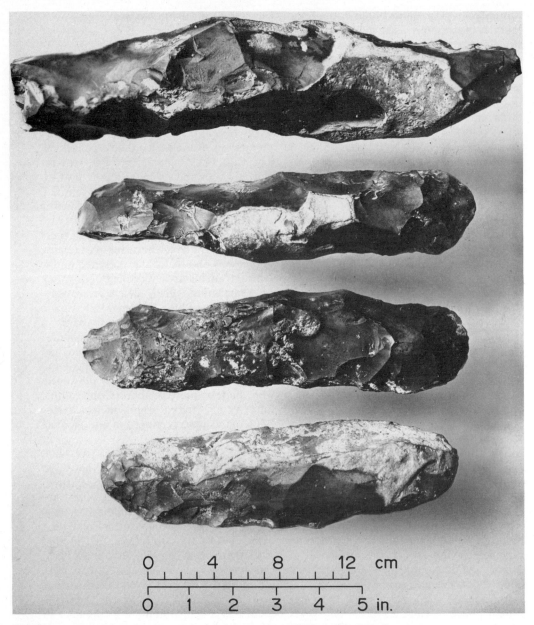

Fig. 8 'Thames picks', large flint 'tranchet' adzes from the river at Richmond and elsewhere

been in the mildest phase of the first half of the Atlantic period. The implements themselves were evidently somewhat earlier, and were probably made towards the end of the Boreal or the beginning of the Atlantic period, about 5000 B.C.

LATER MESOLITHIC PEOPLE OF THE THAMES VALLEY

Of a later date was an important site at Lower Halstow in the Upchurch Marshes, on the Medway estuary. This was overlaid by peat of the Late Atlantic phase, as was shown by the pollen found in it. It belonged to the period after the Mesolithic people of the Thames Valley had been separated from their kinsmen of the North European plain by the rising seas, which had swamped the low-lying land between them and had made Britain an island. The Lower Halstow people continued to follow the old Maglemosean tradition more closely than some of their contemporaries of north-western Europe, who, after the sea had broken in and transformed the Baltic from a freshwater lake into a sea, had gradually adopted a more settled life as sea-shore fishermen and gatherers of shell-fish. The late Mesolithic people of the Medway estuary continued to use pointed micro-liths, gravers and tranchet core axes, but also used tranchet axes made from large flakes. A pebble with the usual hour-glass perforation was also found there.

The most characteristic tool of this later Mesolithic culture of the Thames Valley, however, was the so-called *Thames pick,* really a heavy tranchet core adze that was long, narrow and thick, and was usually roughly lozenge-shaped or triangular in section (*fig. 8*). Great numbers have been dredged from the bed of the Thames, and found on the surface in its basin, while others have been found at Seaford in Sussex. This rather specialized tool of the later Mesolithic forest people was presumably used for working heavy timber. It could have been used for many purposes, and would, for example, have been well suited for hollowing a dug-out canoe by chipping away the interior of a tree trunk. It may be significant that these heavy tranchet adzes have mostly been found near the Thames or sea-shore, where craft of this kind would have been particularly useful. Dug-out canoes seem to have been made by the Maglemoseans even in Boreal times, since an example from Pesse in Holland has been dated to about 6250 B.C. by radio-carbon analysis. In our own region, a Mesolithic date has been suggested for a dug-out boat found in shelly marl beneath five feet of peat at Sewardstone near Chingford. This was made from a solid trunk of oak, and was about 13 ft long. It would, no doubt, have been propelled by wooden paddles like the one found on the famous early Mesolithic site at Star Carr in Yorkshire.

THE USE OF BONE AND ANTLER

Star Carr gives a much fuller picture of Mesolithic life than any occupied area in our region, because organic material, such as antler, bone, and even wood, was well preserved there. Barbed spear-points, and the heads of axes and adzes perforated for hafting were made of red-deer and elk antler at Star Carr, as on Continental Maglemosean sites. Similar tools are not uncommon in our region, although they have not yet been found archaeologically associated with the characteristic flint industry. Most, in fact, are unstratified finds from the Thames or its tributaries, many of them having been found while dredging the river. A typical barbed bone point of the kind used as a spear-head both

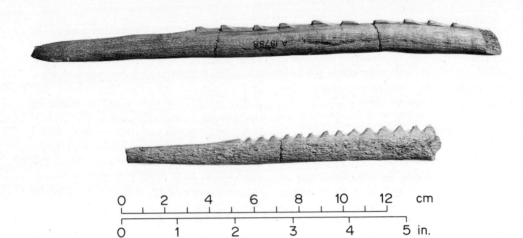

Fig. 9 Mesolithic barbed spear-heads of bone from the Thames at Battersea (above) and Wandsworth

in hunting and fishing, was found at Battersea, and there is another from Wandsworth (*fig. 9*). The commonest bone and antler tools of Mesolithic type that are found in the Thames, however, are implements with shaft-holes for hafting, sometimes with edges sharpened by grinding like those of the Baltic. One example of this kind from Hammersmith had its original handle wedged in the shaft-hole. Some were not sharpened themselves, but had sockets which originally held stone adze-or axe-blades, like a perforated antler implement from Twickenham; while others, like one from Isleworth made from the thick crown of an antler, were evidently merely hammers. A similar hammer from Teddington is decorated with a net-like pattern made by pecking and rubbing, as is an antler socket believed to be from Brentford; but both, though in a Mesolithic tradition, may belong to a later period. There is little doubt, however, about the date of a fine decorated holder for an adze blade from Hammersmith, made from the leg-bone of a wild ox, and perforated for hafting (*fig. 10a*). This object, now in the British Museum, is carved with a parallel zig-zag ornament of the kind found among the Mesolithic people of the Baltic. It may have had some magical significance or may have been merely an owner's mark, but whatever its meaning, it stands almost alone as an undoubted example of the art of Mesolithic Britain.

CAMPS OF MESOLITHIC HUNTERS

To the dwellers on the Thames and its larger tributaries, fishing was probably at least as important as hunting, and their way of life remained close to that of the fen people of north-western Europe, from whom they had come. To the south and south-west of our region, however, were Mesolithic communities whose environment was very different, and who must have obtained their food mainly by hunting the wild animals of the forest of the Weald and the more open country on its fringes. They themselves preferred to camp in the dry sandy areas of the zone of Greensand between the North Downs, where they could obtain flint for their tools, and the Wealden forest itself. Some sites seem to

16

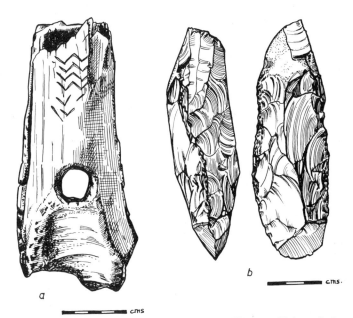

Fig. 10 Decorated bone holder for a flint adze from Hammersmith, and flint axe with 'tranchet' cutting edge from Erith

have been semi-permanent, with pit-dwellings (as at Farnham) while others were merely hunters' camps, but all were probably only used seasonally. A greater variety of microliths was made by these people, who no doubt used a number of specialized hunting weapons, for which some of these tiny flints may have served as barbs. Some microliths were of geometric forms, and in their use of these, as in their preference for open sandy sites, the Mesolithic people of the Weald show relationship to their contemporaries of Belgium and France. They also used the tranchet axes and perforated pebbles of Maglemosean origin, however, and these are likely to have been introduced by contact with the people of the Thames Estuary or Valley.

Penetration to the south by way of the Medway is shown by a site at Addington in Kent, where a fragment of a pebble mace-head was found with tranchet axes

and microliths, sealed beneath peat of the Atlantic period. There are also suggestions of connections between the flourishing Mesolithic communities of the north-west Weald and the Middle Thames along the streams of the Wey and Mole. A Mesolithic floor was found in clay silt beside the latter

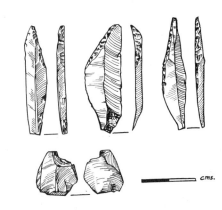

Fig. 11 Flint microliths from Sandown Park, Esher

17

river at Leatherhead, and the material from it included a tranchet axe. Nearer the Thames is a site on dry sandy ground 100 ft above the Mole in The Warren, Sandown Park, Esher, where simple microliths and scrapers have been found (*fig. 11*). Farther east another line of penetration is suggested by a series of open sites where surface finds have been made on Barnes Common, Wimbledon Common, Ham Common, Old Malden and Ewell. Here again, the sites are on dry sand or gravel, near small feeders of the Thames—the Beverley Brook and the Hogsmill River.

HUNTERS AND FOOD-GATHERERS

The Mesolithic hunters might wander widely in search of game, but returned to pitch their camps near a convenient water supply. Here they skinned and cut up the day's kill, and here they repaired their weapons with new flint points and barbs. It is on these camping sites, therefore, that their stone tools remain, usually as the only indication of the hunters' former presence. The worked flints may be found in great numbers, but each site was probably occupied at any one time by only a very few individuals. Hunting groups must, in fact, have been smaller than in the Old Stone Age, when the hunting of really big game required co-operative effort, and a single success could provide food for a considerable number. Some camps were no doubt used again and again, perhaps over a very long period, though never for very long at a time. With the dog as their only domestic animal, and without any knowledge of agriculture, these people were entirely dependent on the wild animals and fish that they could catch, and the edible wild plants that they could find; so that the quest for food to remain alive must have

required constant movement, but movement that probably fell into a regular seasonal pattern. It must also have required an intimate knowledge of the habits of wild creatures and the opportunities offered by the various kinds of country at different times in the year.

In this respect the way of life of the Mesolithic people was basically the same as that of their predecessors throughout the long ages of the Palaeolithic period—or, for that matter, of modern people, such as the Eskimo, the Australian Aborigines, the Bushmen of the Kalahari, and some jungle-dwellers of Central Africa, India, Malaya and Indonesia, who remain at the same primitive stage of culture today. Modern hunters and food-gatherers must necessarily live in small nomadic groups, but this does not prevent them from developing elaborate magical rites and enriching their lives with ceremonial. A number of antler frontlets prepared for use as head-dresses, found at Star Carr in Yorkshire, may have been worn by hunters as decoys, but may equally well have been worn by masked dancers in a ritual performance. Similarly, some modern primitive people use complex and ingenious hunting weapons and fishing appliances—harpoons and harpoon arrows, poisoned darts, boomerangs, bolases and the like, as well as traps and snares of many kinds. Very little archaeological evidence would survive to indicate ingenuity of this kind, and it would be reasonable to credit our Mesolithic people with no less skill and invention. That their ancestors had successfully adapted to a complete change of environment, from the open steppes and tundra to the more difficult hunting conditions of the forests, suggests considerable natural ability. We have archaeological evidence for one major invention—the tranchet axe or adze; there must have been many others, connected with the all important business of hunting and fishing, that have vanished without trace. The material culture brought by the Maglemoseans to Britain was therefore probably much richer than can be deduced from the worked flints and bones that now survive.

Most of the animals hunted by the Mesolithic people of our region can still be found in Europe; and, although no human remains that are certainly of this period have yet been found in Britain, there is no doubt from Continental evidence, that, unlike the earlier hunters of the Thames Valley, these were men of the modern type. A Mesolithic man brought back to life and dressed in modern clothes would attract no special attention today.

The Mesolithic hunters and fishermen were probably few in number, and we do not know what happened to them eventually. It is quite possible that their descendants continued to live on the banks of the Thames for centuries after a more advanced way of life had been adopted. Farming, as we shall see, was introduced from overseas, and this made possible the growth of larger communities, in which trade and specialized skills could flourish. Hunting became less important, but fishermen no doubt continued to gain their living from what could be described 5000 years later as 'the fishfull river of Thames'.

4 Primitive Farmers of the New Stone Age

THE BEGINNING OF FARMING

While the Mesolithic people of north-west Europe were adapting themselves to hunting in the recently grown forests, farther east other hunters and food-gatherers were beginning to develop farming—not a single invention, but a story of gradually increasing control of their food supply by various peoples of western Asia. Reapers of wild corn learnt to sow it; hunters of wild goats learnt to herd them; and the new knowledge, together with the necessary seed and stock, passed from one people to another. As a result the full Neolithic (New Stone Age) way of life developed. An economy based on mixed farming, in which corn was grown, and oxen, goats, sheep and pigs were bred, made possible the growth of larger communities, and gave some leisure from the quest for food. Crafts, including the making of pottery, developed and trade became important. A useful new tool was the stone axe that was finally shaped and sharpened by grinding and polishing.

The new way of life reached Britain before 3,500 B.C. (See note on dating, p. viii)

It was brought by immigrants, who probably carried their cattle across the Channel in large skin boats. We do not yet know where they came from, or where they first landed, but their known settlements are mainly on the chalk downs of Wessex and Sussex, which provided easily cleared land for grazing and cultivation, and also plenty of flint for tool-making. Here they constructed their mysterious 'causewayed camps'—rings of ditches interrupted by undug causeways, but with continuous inner banks, encircling a central enclosure. When these camps were first found, they were thought to be fortified villages, but actual hut sites were hard to find, and nearly all the rubbish of occupation, such as animal bones and broken pottery, came from the ditches. It was suggested, therefore, that they were seasonal meeting-

places, and that the central part was used as an enclosure for the cattle, possibly herded for an autumn slaughtering to reduce their number before winter, when there would be little food for them. More recently it has been pointed out that the causewayed camps are in some respects similar to the later Neolithic circular *henge* monuments, the purpose of which must be religious, and it has been suggested that they were used in some kind of tribal ritual.

STAINES CAUSEWAYED CAMP

Until 1960, nobody suspected the existence of any causewayed camp in the London region, although one lay just beyond our northern limit in the Chilterns. Eleven of the thirteen examples then known were on the chalk uplands; and although one had

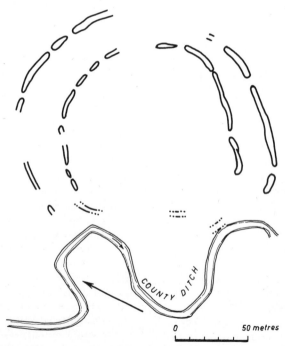

Fig. 12 Plan of Staines Neolithic causewayed camp

been found on the gravel of the Thames Valley, this was far away on the Upper Thames at Abingdon, near Oxford. Study of an air photograph, however, showed faint traces of two concentric interrupted ditches, almost obliterated by ploughing, near Yeoveney Lodge, about a mile N.W. of Staines. The earthwork, which is now destroyed, covered an area of 5½ acres on a low-lying site between two small tributaries of the Thames, partly on gravel and partly on alluvium. Excavation was carried out, and the ditches were found to be of the usual causewayed flat-bottomed type (*fig. 12*). In the silt of their fill, a great quantity of pottery was found of the simple, earlier Neolithic kind. This ware, which consists mainly of round-bottomed bowls with little decoration, has many local variations. Only in one place, in a higher level of the filling of the outer ditch, was any late Neolithic pottery found. The broken fragments were usually in small piles at all levels of the ditch-silt, as if they had been swept there from hut floors throughout the period of the silting.

Animal bones were also found in the ditches, usually in separate dumps, and from one of these came a complete polished flint axe. Shoulder-blades and other meat bones of oxen were found, but there was very little deer antler, so that hunting seems to have been much less important than farming. Two human skulls and part of a forearm, found among the animal bones and domestic rubbish in the outer ditch, suggest that these Neolithic people may have been cannibals. Similar finds have been made in several causewayed camps, but there are other possible explanations, such as head-hunting or tomb robbing for magical purposes.

Flint implements found included axes both completely and partly polished, leaf-shaped arrowheads, scrapers, knife-blades and saws (flakes with finely notched edges). The flint used was not from the local gravels, but was probably obtained by trade from the distant chalk-lands, as was shown by the discovery of several large nodules that are likely to have come from the chalk. Evidence of trade with places even farther away is given by a chip of a greenstone axe, which must have come from the Lake District.

Corn was ground into flour by rubbing it with a grinding-stone against a larger stone with a flattish or slightly concave surface, using a to-and-fro movement. The presence of smoothed stones of these kinds is the only indication that the inhabitants grew corn as well as herding cattle.

An important discovery was a great number of small pits with occasional post-holes in the interior of the camp, showing that the central portion was not just a corral for cattle, but was occupied by the tribesmen themselves. Near the middle was a straight trench for a wooden fence or wall, about 70 ft long, which might be part of a long rectangular building. All this, together with the indication of continuous occupation during the silting of the ditch, suggests that the Staines causewayed camp at least may have been a place of permanent settlement. It may of course also have been a religious centre. If, in fact, this was a tribal headquarters, it would naturally have been the place where the ceremonies and ritual that bound the tribe together would have taken place.

Are there any more undiscovered causewayed camps in the London region? One other is at least suspected. Air photographs show what appear to be the characteristic broken rings of ditches in land that is at present under cultivation at East Bedfont, about 3 miles east of the Staines camp, and just south of London

Airport. The site is soon to be developed, and it is very much to be hoped that an opportunity will be given for a full archaeological excavation before the buried ditches are swept away. This may well have been the fate of other causewayed camps now lost under the built-up area of Greater London. There would probably have been no visible trace at ground level to attract attention before the use of air photography, which can reveal buried ditches and banks by indicating variation in the growth of crops. These grow taller over the deep soil in a ditch, and shorter over the shallow soil above a bank, so that the lines of ploughed-out earthworks can be picked out from the air, though they are not identifiable from the ground.

EARLY NEOLITHIC SETTLERS IN THE THAMES VALLEY

Since the early Neolithic people settled near Staines, there is no reason at all why they should not have made use of similar gravels throughout the Thames Valley. So far, however, their simple bag-shaped or shouldered pottery has been found only well to the west of Central London. A complete bowl has been dredged from the Thames near Kew Bridge (*fig. 13a*); and fragments have been found with flint flakes and animal bones in the beds of small streams during recent excavations at Kingston and Twickenham. Pottery believed to be early Neolithic and worked flints were found even more recently in Brentford. In each of these excavations the Neolithic occupation was a chance discovery where it had not been expected. Equally suitable sites, with land that could easily be cleared for farming on the gravels, and a convenient water supply from shallow streams, abound in the Thames Valley, and many more such finds may be made. The pottery of the early Neolithic people is

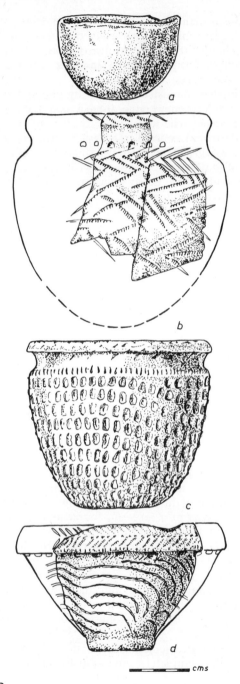

inconspicuous, with little decoration, and might therefore be overlooked if found by non-archaeologists, so that its distribution may be much wider than we now know. It is even possible that the Thames Valley may prove to have been one of their routes into Britain, although on present evidence it seems more likely that they came to the London region from Wessex, gradually moving downstream, but perhaps not reaching the lower part of the Valley.

LATER NEOLITHIC OCCUPATION

In later Neolithic times, after about 3000 B.C., however, there was certainly occupation on the lower Thames and its tributaries. The site that has given its name to the earlier pottery of this period is in fact the little stream of the Ebbsfleet, which flows into the Thames at Northfleet, near Gravesend. In the sandy silt of the stream-bed were found fragments of well-baked handmade pottery together with flint flakes. Most of the pots represented here had slightly concave necks, rather weak shoulders, and rounded bases. A number were decorated with criss-cross lines scratched on the rims, or with marks made by the potter's fingernail or finger-tip on the necks, and one rim was ornamented with impressions of a piece of cord (cf fig. 13b). Ebbsfleet ware is an early variety of a large class of British Neolithic pottery often called Peterborough ware, which is found mostly in southern and eastern England, and seems to have a general relationship with the early pottery of Scandinavia. It is believed, however, that Ebbsfleet ware is a local development from

Fig. 13 Neolithic pottery, (a) from Kew Bridge
    (b) Ebbsfleet ware from Mortlake,
    (c) Mortlake ware from Heathrow,
    (d) Fengate ware from Hammersmith (?)

earlier British Neolithic pottery rather than a new type introduced by settlers from Northern Europe. Later it developed, probably locally, into Mortlake ware (fig. 13c), a variety of Peterborough ware so named because a fine bowl of this style was dredged from the Thames at Mortlake. This Late Neolithic pottery usually has a deeply constricted neck above a shoulder that is often angular, and is decorated over most of its body in a way that imitates basketwork. The ornamentation was made by pressing short lengths of twisted or whipped cord on to the clay so that it looks rather like rows of maggots. Sometimes the end of a bird's bone was used instead. The rim is thickened and often over-hanging, and in its final development (Fengate pottery of about 1700 B.C.) becomes a collar (fig. 13d).

We know very little about the life of these later Neolithic peoples, but sites that they occupied have been excavated at Heathrow during the construction of London Airport, and more recently at Baston Manor, Hayes, near Bromley, Kent. At Heathrow, two pits of this period were found in the gravel within a later (Early Iron Age) earthwork, but there was no definite trace of a Neolithic hut structure. In addition to the usual round decorated bowls (fig. 13c) there was a small oval bowl of a type found in Denmark, where it is thought to be a blubber-lamp. At Hayes, near Bromley, a flint-chipping floor was found, with quantities of flakes and the burnt flints used in primitive cooking. Flint tools included scrapers, knives, a polished axe-head and a leaf-shaped arrow-head. The site must have been in use for a long time, since all three of the main Peterborough types of pottery were found. Pottery mid-way between the Ebbsfleet and Mortlake styles was found at Thorpe in Surrey, across the river from Staines; and both varieties have been found at Yiewsley, West Drayton. Ebbsfleet ware has also been found, together with many flint flakes and tools, in the neighbourhood of Sefton Street, Putney.

A very distinctive type of Late Neolithic pottery is known as *Grooved* or *Rinyo-Clacton* ware (after sites at Rinyo in Orkney and Clacton in Essex where it has been found). This has flat bases and is decorated over much of its surface with grooves and dots, making up chevron, triangular and lozenge-shaped patterns. Its main distribution in southern Britain extends from Wessex to East Anglia across the northern edge of our region, where it has been found on the ditch floor of Waulud's Bank, a semi-circular earthwork at the source of the river Lea. It seems to be rare on the Thames, but has been tentatively identified among the pottery fragments from the river at Strand-on-the-Green and Hammersmith, and from excavations at Putney.

NEOLITHIC TOOLS

A great number of flint and stone tools of the Neolithic period have been found in the London region, many of them in the Thames (*fig. 14*). They do not necessarily indicate that Neolithic people lived in the neighbourhood where they were found, since they could have been lost by Neolithic travellers, many of whom journeyed along the river by boat. This is especially true of the most typical tools of the period, the ground and polished axes, for these were objects of trade. Flint axes probably came from the mines on the South Downs and in East Anglia, as well as from East Horsley on the North Downs and Pitstone Hill in the Chilterns, where flint-miners' shafts have been identified. A hoard of 5 flint axes found in a garden at Bexleyheath, Kent, and another at Canewdon, Essex, may well have been the stocks of travelling merchants. In later Neolithic times axes of stone other than flint came from Cornwall, Wales and the Lake District, and their sources can be identified by microscopic examination of thin sections taken from them. Numbers of axes have been found in or near those parts of the river where

Fig. 14 Neolithic polished flint axe from Staines, with lighter band showing where it was hafted.

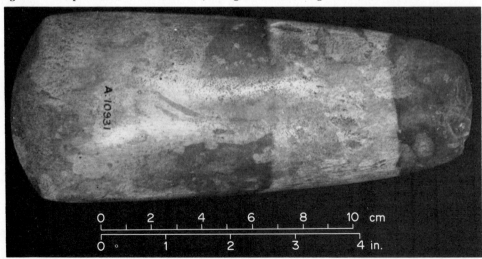

24

Neolithic pottery occurs; at Staines near the causewayed camp, from Kingston to Twickenham, Isleworth to Kew, and Mortlake to Hammersmith. There were comparatively few below Chelsea Bridge, except in the older parts of London, where quite a number have been found. This may mean that there was Neolithic occupation in the City and Westminster or Holborn, and that the small quantities of inconspicuous Neolithic pottery have passed unnoticed in the great mass of later finds. There is unfortunately another possible explanation. Neolithic axes are fairly striking objects, and before their real origin was understood were thought to be thunderbolts. As such they were believed to have magical powers, and were therefore collected and taken home by much later Londoners. One was in fact found on an Anglo-Saxon floor in Whitehall, associated with pottery of the 9th century A.D. There is no reason why central London should not have been occupied in Neolithic times, but we need more definite evidence before we can be sure that it was.

Leaf-shaped arrow-heads, a type which continued in use throughout Neolithic times, have been found at Twickenham, Richmond, Brentford, Acton, Mortlake, Putney and Wandsworth, in addition to the sites already mentioned. They are usually beautifully chipped by removing tiny flakes all over their surfaces by pressure, probably with a bone tool. Chisel-edged tranchet arrowheads of Mesolithic ancestry also must have continued in use, as they are known to have done elsewhere. Quite a number of rare disc-shaped or triangular knives with polished edges, probably used in preparing hides, have been found in the Thames Valley. There are also curved flint sickles from Hammersmith, Chelsea, Greenwich and Bexley. Apart from grinding stones at Yeoveney, tools of this kind are the only indication of corn-growing as well as stock-breeding in Neolithic London.

NEOLITHIC TOMBS

Neolithic people elsewhere buried some of their dead in communal tombs beneath long mounds, called long barrows, but with a possible exception on Wimbledon Common none are yet known in our region. Only just beyond the ridge of the North Downs that forms its natural boundary to the south-east in Kent, however, are several Neolithic tombs built of large pieces of local greywether sandstone (sarsens) in the megalithic ('great stone') tradition, found widely along the western seaboard of Europe. Kit's Coty House, beyond the Medway, is the remnant of a rectangular chamber at the end of a long barrow. Part of a long barrow itself remains at Addington, with a line of stones along its edges; and in another buried chamber not far away at Coldrum Farm, were found the remains of at least 22 individuals, believed to be related because of certain family likenesses. They were also fairly typical of the British Neolithic people, being long-headed, short and slightly built, with fine features—very much like the small dark people still to be found in parts of Wales and Cornwall.

THE BEAKER PEOPLE

The closing phase of the Neolithic period and its transition to the Bronze Age were marked by invasions from the Low Countries and Rhineland of people of a different physical type, round-headed and sturdy, who buried their more important dead in individual graves beneath round barrows. They were warriors, skilled in the use of the bow, who tipped their arrows with

Fig 15 Beaker pottery from Erith (a,b) and Mortlake (c)

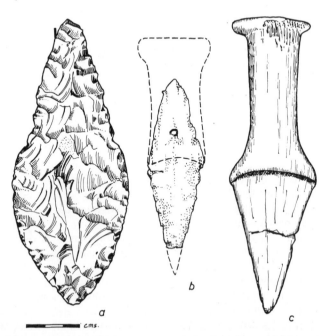

Fig. 16 Daggers of Beaker period from the Thames: (a) flint dagger from Battersea, (b) copper dagger from Mortlake, (c) bone copy of copper dagger

26

barbed flint heads. They also seem to have been hearty drinkers, probably of beer, since a characteristic drinking-vessel or beaker usually accompanied a burial. For this reason they are called the *Beaker People*. Their invasions came in two main waves, extending over several centuries between about 2400 B.C. and 2000 B.C. The second wave was a complicated series of migrations arriving at various times from the Middle Rhine and the coastal region of the Netherlands, and settling in various parts of the British Isles. These movements have recently been worked out by a detailed study of beakers and their decoration with the help of a computer. Some settled in the Thames Estuary and Valley, and a considerable number of beakers and beaker fragments of various types and dates have come from the river itself, especially from the stretch most favoured by prehistoric man between Putney and Brentford, with notable finds at Mortlake (*fig. 15c*). Beaker pottery also occurs near Staines, at Hackney, and near Erith, where two beakers found in a gravel pit were probably from graves (*fig. 15a and b*). On the north side of the Thames Estuary, Beaker settlement seems to have been strong in the neighbourhood of Shoebury-ness, perhaps a point of entry for some of the invaders.

The Beaker people were still essentially Neolithic in their way of life, although the complicated migrations on the Continent that led to their invasion of Britain seem to have been connected with the search for copper. The Beaker invaders therefore may well have introduced metal-working, although they possessed few objects of metal. Apart from the bow, their principal weapon was a finely chipped flint dagger that seems to copy the form of the earliest copper daggers (*fig. 16a*). In Wessex they were sometimes able to obtain the real thing from the Continent or Ireland but it is almost unknown in the London region. There is a copper dagger from the Thames at Mortlake (*fig. 16b*), and analysis suggests that its metal comes from Central Europe. It was therefore probably brought from the Continent by one of the invaders. There is also a copy of a metal dagger in bone from the Thames (*fig. 16c*). The flint daggers, however, are abundant, especially in or near the river between Battersea and Sunbury.

Another weapon of the Beaker people was the polished stone battle-axe, an axe-hammer with a cylindrical hole for a haft. Examples have been found in the Thames at Westminster and in the City, as well as in the more favoured stretch of the river farther upstream. As with the polished axes, such finds do not necessarily indicate local prehistoric occupation, and the only beaker from the City has a doubtful history, but is said to have been found in a Tudor well. The find of a Beaker type barbed arrow-head, with scrapers and other worked flints, immediately above the natural sand in Southwark, however, shows that there was some occupation of the older part of London in this period. Finds of flint daggers suggest that Beaker people also found their way up the Lea valley into north London (Tottenham).

The Late Neolithic people survived long after the Beaker settlements had begun. We do not know whether the invaders became their overlords, or merely traded with them, but there must have been contact between the two peoples. There seems to have been mutual influence between them in pottery decoration, and this is likely to have extended into other fields. Beaker settlements appear to have been mostly of an insubstantial character, but we know little about them, or about the daily life of the people. Although they were probably more concerned with cattle than corn-growing, they apparently grew barley, perhaps mainly for brewing.

5 Smiths, Merchants and Warriors on the Thames

Although the Beaker people were occasional users of copper, the general use of metal did not begin in Britain until the introduction of bronze (copper alloyed with tin) after about 1700 B.C. The exploitation of Cornish tin together with Irish, and probably Welsh, copper and gold led to the development of trade between western Britain and the Continent. Some of this merchandise probably passed down the Thames Valley, and a few flat axes, axes with flanged (raised) edges and grooved daggers of this period have been found in the river, mostly between the Lea and the Wey. There is no clear evidence as yet of metal-working in the London region during this period, and the weapons found might well have been made in Wessex or East Anglia. There is also from the Thames a fine dagger with a decorated bronze hilt that is certainly an import from the Continent, probably from Germany (fig. 18a).

The distinctive Beaker pottery seems to have disappeared, and its makers had probably merged with the native population after losing whatever privileged position they had once held. Pottery of the Early Bronze Age found at Hammersmith and Mortlake included fragments of jars with overhanging rims or collars, elsewhere commonly used as urns for cremations, that are usually buried in round burial mounds—a method of disposal of the dead that was now general. This kind of pottery is closely related in form and ornament (impressions of twisted cord) to the Late Neolithic Fengate ware, itself a development of Mortlake ware. It seems likely, therefore, that the people who made these pots about 1500 B.C. were themselves descendants of the late Neolithic people who had lived in the Thames Valley several centuries earlier. To this period probably belonged the burial mound excavated at Teddington in 1854. A sketch of a bronze dagger is the only illustration of the lost finds, which included a cremation, fragments of a large urn and flint implements. There are other possible burial mounds or barrows on Wimbledon Common and in Richmond Park; and a well-known mound that may be a barrow lies north of Parliament Hill, Hampstead Heath. The name *Tothill*, preserved in Tothill Street, Westminster, may indicate that there was once a similar earthwork there, since there is a reference to 'a mound'

Fig. 17 Pottery bucket urn of Deverel-Rimbury type from Sunbury

in a late Saxon charter giving the boundary of the Abbey land. There is also *Barrow Hill*, Primrose Hill, a site now occupied by a waterworks.

THE MIDDLE BRONZE AGE

In the Middle Bronze Age, between about 1400 and 900 B.C., many new types of bronze weapons were introduced from the Continent, and great development of bronze-working took place in Britain. Unfortunately for archaeologists, a change took place in burial customs about 1400 B.C., and personal possessions were no longer buried with the dead. Since a great part of our knowledge of the Bronze Age comes from a study of finds associated in burials, rather than sites occupied by the living, we do not know much about the pottery of the people who made and used these new weapons. After about 1200 B.C., however, rather crude bucket-shaped, barrel-shaped and rounded pots were in use, sometimes decorated with finger impressions on applied strips of clay (*fig. 17*). This pottery is called *Deverel-Rimbury* after a site in Dorset. Many burial urns of this kind of pottery have been found in cemeteries on Sunbury Common and at Yiewsley, and a smaller number at Acton and (probably) Kingsbury. It used to be thought that this ware was introduced by invaders, but it is now believed to be a British development from Early Bronze Age pottery. There is no evidence that this development took place in the London region, however, and it seems that here the pots were introduced by new arrivals, probably from some other part of Britain. The number of burials found together suggests that the population was now larger than in the Early Bronze Age, and lived a more settled life. Unfortunately it has not yet been possible to investigate any dwelling

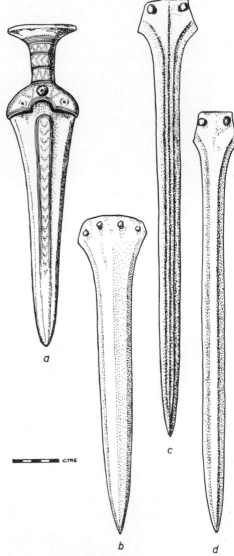

Fig. 18 Bronze Age dagger, dirk and rapiers from the Thames (b) from Ditton (c) Wandsworth, (d) Barnes

sites in the London area, but elsewhere the people who made this pottery are known to have been farmers who kept cattle and sheep, and grew corn in small squarish fields, which they cultivated with the plough. They lived in well-built round huts, often grouped in enclosures.

Our lack of evidence about the daily life in the region during the Middle Bronze Age has compensation in the abundant finds of metal-work of the period, mainly from the Thames. These were mostly new types introduced from the Continent about 1400 B.C., and further developed in Britain. The flanged axe was replaced by the *palstave*, which was hafted like the flanged axe by wedging its butt into the forepart of an elbow-shaped handle, but was provided with a stop-ridge to prevent splitting of the handle (*fig. 19a*). The short dagger was replaced by the longer dirk, which by about 1200 B.C. had developed into the even longer rapier, an elegant thrusting weapon at least 12 inches and often 18-24 inches long (*fig. 18c, d*). It seems clear that metal-working was now being carried on in the London region, although we still lack direct evidence of it in the form of moulds for casting or other datable material from the smiths' workshops. Certain types of dirk and rapier, and also spears with a straight-sided blade and loops at the base of the blade, are, however, so abundant in the Thames near London, compared with their numbers elsewhere, that it seems reasonably certain that they were made locally. Also very common in the London region, though with a wide distribution in S.E. Britain, are leaf-shaped spear-heads with loops on the side of the socket, and palstaves with low flanges. Some at least of these are also likely to have been produced in the region.

A little before 1000 B.C., towards the end of the Middle Bronze Age, there are indications of much closer links with the Continent. Personal ornaments and new types of bronze implements, including notched and tanged razors, were introduced from France and Germany. There

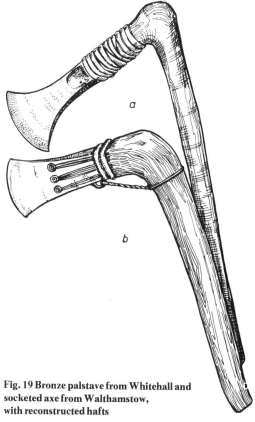

Fig. 19 **Bronze palstave from Whitehall and socketed axe from Walthamstow, with reconstructed hafts**

were also new foreign axes—notably the socketed axe, cast with a hollow socket into which the forepart of the elbow-shaped haft could be wedged (*fig. 19b*). It was to become the characteristic tool of the Late Bronze Age. A formidable new weapon, destined to oust the rapier, also made its first appearance in Britain. This was the bronze slashing sword, with the hilt cast in one piece with the blade (unlike the rapier, in which it was riveted on), and with a leaf-shaped blade. With its greater weight in the lower part of the blade, it was especially intended for cutting strokes, but could, of course, be used for stabbing as well. For several centuries, the Thames

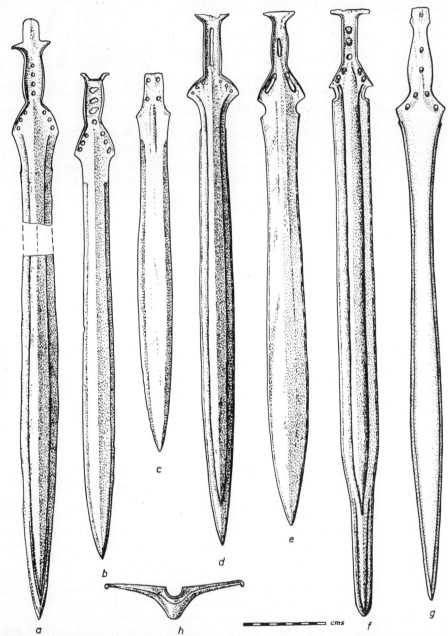

Fig. 20 Bronze swords from the Thames: *imported* —(a) **Battersea,** (b) **Hammersmith,** (f), (g) **Brentford:** *local*—(c) **Chelsea,** (d) **Hammersmith,** (e) **Battersea**

Valley with south east Britain, through its links with the Continent, now remained in advance of the rest of the country in the introduction of new types of equipment. The Thames was the main entry for this trade, and imported swords of the earliest type, originating in the Upper Rhine Valley and Switzerland, as can be deduced from the great concentration found there, are in Britain found only in the Thames Valley between Brentford and Barking (*fig. 20a, b*).

The new swords were copied enthusiastically by the local smiths, with various small changes in design. (*fig. 20, c-e*). One type of sword, probably made in the London region, where it is most commonly found, also occurs in Ireland, with which there seem to have been trade links by way of the Bristol Channel.

THE INDUSTRIAL REVOLUTION OF THE LATE BRONZE AGE

Swords, socketed axes, spears made with rivet-holes for fixing to their shafts, and many other types of Continental origin were made in abundance, almost certainly locally, through the Late Bronze Age, which is marked by new methods in metal-working and a great increase of production. The use of bronze deliberately alloyed with a considerable proportion of lead is the characteristic feature of this 'industrial revolution', which began in S.E. Britain between 1000 and 900 B.C. It is not clear what advantage the new alloy gave, apart from lowering the melting point. The actual quality of the metal is likely to have been poorer, so perhaps the real attraction was cheapness, in the sense that more weapons could be produced from the same amount of copper and tin. The craftsman as well as the warrior was served, and chisels, gouges and hammers were produced, as also were cauldrons made by riveting together sheets of beaten bronze.

There is now for the first time definite evidence of local metal-working in a number of hoards of material from bronze-smiths' workshops. One from Southall contained a mould for casting a socketed axe, as did another from Beddington: others from Kingston and Croydon included copper 'cakes' produced by running the molten metal into bowls: and one from Kensington contained a 'jet' of waste metal left as a residue after pouring the bronze into a mould. Socketed axes were associated with them all.

Throughout the Late Bronze Age there was close contact with the Continent, and some hoards—one from Bexleyheath, for example—contain material from western France. French types include winged axes and swords with a narrowed tip, called 'carp's tongue' swords (*fig. 20f*). There are also socketed axes, rather square in section, from Brittany. Continued contact with the mineral wealth of Ireland is suggested by the seventeen gold bracelets found near Bexley, apparently in hut sites that were unfortunately not recorded. Right at the end of the period, after about 650 B.C., new influences from Central Europe reached the Thames Valley, showing the first contact with the *Hallstatt* people (named after a site in Austria) who introduced the knowledge of iron-working to Western Europe. The earliest indications of their presence in Britain, however, are bronze swords with shapely blades of Hallstatt type (*fig. 20g*); and bronze chapes or caps for the ends of their scabbards, with distinctive projecting wings, so that a mounted swordsman could steady his scabbard with his left foot when he drew his sword, leaving his left hand free to hold the reins (*fig. 20h*). Both are commonly found in the Lower Thames, and were probably brought into Britain by this route. We do not know whether foreign weapons were introduced by hostile invaders, immigrant smiths, peaceful traders, or envoys bearing gifts. A large-scale invasion can probably be ruled out, however, as other features of Hallstatt culture do not seem to occur. As with the earlier bronze swords, recognizable local copies of the new types were soon being made, almost certainly in the London region where they are most commonly found. These rather inferior Thames swords were actually exported to the Continent, where they have a widely scattered distribution, extending from Brittany to Denmark, and up the Rhine as far as Württemberg in Germany.

WEAPONS IN THE THAMES

The abundance of Bronze Age weapons in the Thames between Marlow and the estuary, and their great concentration in the part of the river that flows through the western half of Greater London, cannot easily be explained. It is unlikely that they came from dwelling-sites now submerged as a result of changes in the course of the river and the rise in the water level, although such sites are known to exist. These changes took place gradually, however, and the occupants must usually have had plenty of time to get away with their valued possessions.

A succession of battles extending over centuries for the same stretch of river might account for these finds, and would be explicable if the river not only formed a tribal boundary, but was also a valuable prize to be won, because it gave control of a useful trade route. It certainly gave access to the Continent, at a time when the importance of bronze made the distribution of tin and copper from the western parts of the British Isles a flourishing trade. Fighting across the river would suggest that it could be forded in the same place, and

regular crossing-places in West London were no doubt linked by land tracks with the Icknield Way, an important ancient route which ran along the crest of the Chilterns between Wessex and East Anglia, and with the equally important and ancient Pilgrims' Way that similarly followed the high ground of the North Downs from Wessex to the Straits of Dover. The advantages of London as a rather diffuse centre of communications by water and land may therefore already have been appreciated, centuries before the Romans concentrated them on a point a little further downstream by building a bridge there.

Not all the Bronze Age finds from the Thames—even the weapons—need have been lost in battle. Many may have been dropped in the water by accident, and others may well have been deliberately offered to a river deity, in accordance with a custom that certainly existed among the later Celtic people of the Early Iron Age. It may be significant that the Bronze Age shields, of which several have been found in the Thames at London, seem to have been decorative ceremonial objects, incapable of resisting the slash of a bronze sword. It has also been noted that on the Continent weapons of this period are usually found in warriors' graves, and this is never the case in Britain. Does this mean that the dead warrior's weapons were instead given to the river, as King Arthur's sword in the legend was hurled into a lake?

Like battles, however, accidental losses and religious ceremonies are more likely to have taken place where the river was easily reached and frequently crossed. The importance of this concentration of finds is therefore that it shows that this stretch of the Thames had already become a natural meeting-place, whether for trade, battle, religious ritual—or all three purposes.

The introduction of iron shortly before 500 B.C. must in time have affected the trade of the Thames Valley, since the new metal could be found locally almost everywhere. Iron, however, was used mainly for the plainer tools and weapons, while bronze

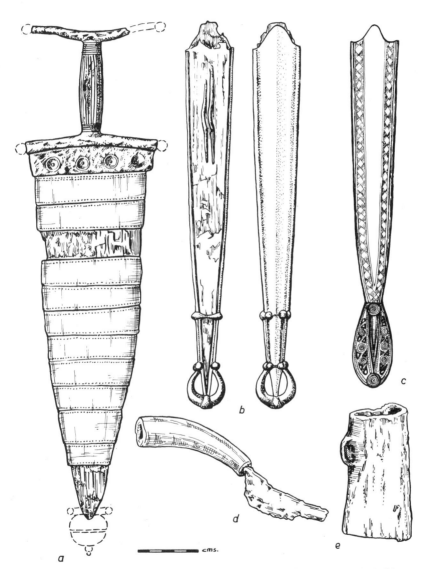

a

b

c

d

e

cms.

Fig. 21 Early Iron Age daggers and tools from the Thames: (a) **Mortlake,** (b), (c) **Wandsworth,** (d) **Brentford,** (e) **Kew**

was still used for the more decorative objects, and for such things as cauldrons. Iron socketed axes were made in the later Bronze Age style, (*fig. 21e*) as well as iron sickles, knives and daggers. There is also a sword from the Thames at London with projections like antennae from the pommel, in the Hallstatt style. Iron daggers were provided with elaborate bronze sheaths which had ring-like terminals. Some of these scabbards are engraved with simple decoration, in which an early form of Celtic curvilinear art can be recognized in several instances (*fig. 21c*). Experts are of the opinion that these daggers from the Thames are of local workmanship, since they show peculiarities seldom found elsewhere, such as twin loops for the attachment of the sheath (*fig. 21b*). They have been dated, from their similarity to types in the Continental sequence, to between about 550 and 300 B.C., when metal-working in the London area seems already to have existed for a thousand years. New knowledge and fashions had been introduced from the Continent, but it is conceivable that many of the traditions of the craft had been handed down locally, and descendants of native Bronze Age smiths may even have been responsible for some of the first tentative attempts in Britain at the new Continental style of art (named *La Tène* after a site in western Switzerland).

Luxury daggers imply the existence of a wealthy ruling class of warrior aristocrats, who need not necessarily have been recent invaders. New types of pottery, however, suggest that there may have been a movement of people into the region, perhaps down the Thames from Wessex rather than directly from the Continent.

LIFE IN THE BRONZE AGE AND EARLY IRON AGE

It must be admitted that we have no clear idea from local evidence of the way of life of the people of the London region in the Bronze Age and the greater part of the pre-Roman Iron Age—that is between about 1700 B.C. and the time of Caesar, when the first glimmering light of history falls on the Thames Valley. Farming obviously continued, with bronze and later iron sickles indicating that the farmers also gained benefits from the new technologies of metal-working. Animal bones from an Early Iron Age occupation site at Heathrow show that oxen, pigs, goats and sheep were farmed, as in the Neolithic period.

Pottery, the development of which can be traced locally from the Late Neolithic to the Middle Bronze Age, becomes something of a mystery in the Late Bronze Age. This period, between about 1000 and 600 B.C. is known to us at present only by its bronze tools and weapons, found in abundance in the Thames. As no occupation sites or burials of the late Bronze Age have yet been recorded, we do not know what pottery was used—or indeed anything else about the life of the people who used these weapons. New shapes of pottery, mostly with shoulders, were introduced from the Continent, however, and are associated with the early use of iron; it is possible that some of these forms may already have arrived in the Late Bronze Age. A distinctive type of ware that was coloured red with haematite (oxide of iron), in a fashion introduced from France about 500 B.C., occurs in our region, but its distribution suggests that the idea was brought down the Thames from the west rather than directly from the Continent.

EARLY IRON AGE SETTLEMENT AT HEATHROW

Occupation sites of the earlier part of the pre-Roman Iron Age are less elusive than those of the Bronze Age, and are known at

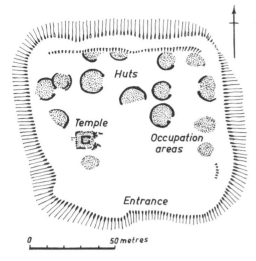

Enfield, Shepperton and Brentford on the north side of the river, and at Esher, Epsom, Bagshot, Thorpe, Wisley and Carshalton on the south side. The only one that has been sufficiently excavated to give a true picture of its nature, however, is the earthwork known as 'Caesar's Camp' at Heathrow, Harmondsworth, destroyed in the construction of London Airport. This was an enclosure defended by a bank and ditch, containing in its northern part eleven circular hut-sites (*fig. 22*). It can hardly be described as a village, but presumably contained several related households. The southern part contained no buildings, and was probably used as a farmyard and enclosure for cattle. This was no ordinary farm, however, for on the western side was a remarkable rectangular building that can

Fig. 22 Plan of Early Iron Age hamlet, Heathrow, after survey by W.F. Grimes

Fig. 23 Reconstruction of Early Iron Age hamlet at Heathrow by Alan Sorrell

only have been a temple. It consisted of a central shrine, which must have had solid wooden walls, enclosed by an outer rectangle of thick wooden posts. It was probably covered by a thatched roof, that extended downwards from a central ridge-pole to the outer posts. This building must have been very like a classical Greek temple, with the stone columns replaced by wooden posts, and the stone-walled sanctuary by a structure like a log cabin (*fig. 23*). The Celtic world had many contacts with the Greeks, and it is quite likely that this type of temple was in fact copied from those of the Mediterranean.

After about 300 B.C. the London region seems to have lost the ascendancy which it had enjoyed for the previous thousand years. During most of that period, as we have seen, new styles of weapon and metalwork introduced from the Continent, and local copies of them, are remarkably concentrated on the Lower Thames. This seems to be no longer the case between about 300 and 100 B.C., for there are few finds that can be definitely dated to this period. Too much weight should not be given to negative evidence of this kind, and occupation certainly continued. The comparative scarcity of metalwork from the river, however, probably indicates a decline of trade. This might be due partly to the lessening demand for British bronze on the Continent, and partly to the disruption resulting from the movements of peoples during this period.

6 The Eve of the Roman Conquest

The later part of the pre-Roman Iron Age in Britain was a disturbed period of invasion and the movement of peoples. These led to the construction of hill-forts which could serve as refuges in time of trouble, and into which cattle could be driven for protection against raiders. Some, though probably not all, were permanently occupied. The earlier forts consist of a single outer ditch and inner bank, originally faced with a timber wall, which was held back against the bank with wooden tie-beams. The entrance is usually simple. Sometimes a slighter bank was also thrown up on the outside of the ditch, as with the so-called 'Caesar's Camp' on Wimbledon Common, tentatively dated by pottery found in excavation to about the 3rd century B.C. (*fig. 24*). This earthwork is circular and encloses an area of about 12 acres. The defences do not now look very formidable, but the ditch was originally more than 12 ft deep and 30 to 40 ft wide, while the rampart was faced front and back with timber walls.

Another hill-fort that was probably first occupied in the 3rd century B.C. is on St George's Hill, Weybridge, where it is now partly covered by a housing estate. This hill-fort was also used, and probably reconstructed, in the half-century before the Roman conquest.

Fig. 24 Aerial photograph of 'Caesar's Camp' on Wimbledon Common

North of the Thames, a simple hill-fort, probably consisting of a single bank and ditch, surrounds the churchyard and church of St John, at Danbury, east of Chelmsford. In Greater London itself, there seems to have been a similar relationship between an ancient earthwork and a later church at Kingsbury, where the old church of St Andrew is said to have been encircled by a rampart in the 18th century. It will be noticed that the site of an Early Iron Age hill-fort is often indicated by the name-ending of 'bury', from an Old English word meaning a fortified place. Another example in Essex is Ambresbury Banks, south-west of Epping, where excavation showed that the ditch was V-shaped and 10 ft deep. Loughton Camp, also in Epping Forest, likewise has a single bank and ditch in the earlier style, but both of these Epping forts probably belong to the 2nd or 1st century B.C.

A hill-fort in Holwood Park, Keston, near Bromley, Kent, is more complicated, with a double bank and ditch on the west side, and a single on the north. The remaining sides have been destroyed. The entrance on the west side has its banks turned in slightly to protect the passage into the fort. Elsewhere hill-forts with multiple defences seem to be later than those with a single rampart, and the Keston earthwork

39

is unlikely to be earlier than the 2nd century B.C. On the north side of the Thames there are forts with two banks and ditches at Walbury Camp, Essex (near Bishops Stortford) and at The Aubreys near Redbourn, Hertfordshire—the latter being a lowland fort commanding the River Ver. Neither is likely to be very early. At Cholesbury in the Chilterns, just south of Tring, is a hill-fort with two banks and ditches on the north side and three on the south. Excavation has shown that it was probably reconstructed in the 2nd century B.C., and re-fortified in the 1st A.D.

At least one hill-fort is of very early date, and was occupied in the transitional period between the Bronze Age and Early Iron Age, about 600 B.C. This is Ivinghoe Beacon in the Chilterns, where Late Bronze Age metal objects, including a razor and sword fragments, were found. A hill-fort at Carshalton Hospital, may be almost as early, since the lower fill of its ditch contained pottery like that from Ivinghoe.

Most of these earthworks, however, belong to the period after about 300 B.C., when new fashions in ornament and pottery were reaching Southern Britain from Northern France. These were originally derived from the La Tène culture, named after a famous site in Switzerland, but in Britain the new phase is often called *Iron Age B*, to distinguish it from the *Iron Age A* culture that was already established. It is uncertain whether these new fashions were introduced by invasion or trading contacts, but there do seem to have been movements of peoples and a general feeling of insecurity, which led to the construction of hill-forts about this time.

BELGIC INVASIONS

Some of our hill-forts were probably built and others refortified, however, at a later date, when the London region was directly affected by a series of invasions of a warlike people from north-east Gaul called the Belgae. They do not themselves seem to have been builders of hill-forts, though they sometimes took possession of them, but preferred to defend their territory with long ditches and embankments.

The Belgae were partly of Celtic and partly of German origin, and had a genius for political organization, mainly based on a well-developed system of kingship. Their rulers seem to have had tremendous prestige, which enabled them to become overlords to tribes with quite different traditions. Comparatively small numbers of Belgae, led by one of their kings, seem to have been able to take over a territory with its inhabitants, and to impose on it their distinctive way of life, called for convenience the *Iron Age C* culture. It is an indication of the advanced political and economic development of the Belgae that their kings actually issued coins. These were the first British coins, although the later Iron Age B people in the west of England were probably already using iron currency bars of standard weights.

The study of the various types of Belgic coin and their distribution has made it possible to trace the movements in Britain of the successive waves of Iron Age C invaders. The earlier types are copies—or rather copies of copies many times removed—of the gold stater of Philip II of Macedon, which had the head of Apollo on one side and a chariot on the other. Both subjects became less and less realistic, and gradually disintegrated into the curls and pellets of Celtic ornament, so that the eventual result was two patterns that appear to be almost meaningless. These patterns themselves became standardized in various ways as the design of a particular tribe or area. Each type has a limited distribution, and the coins are therefore believed to have circulated mainly within

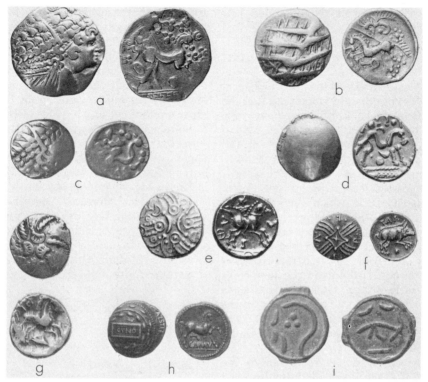

Fig. 25 Pre-Roman coins: (a–e), (g), **gold;** (f) **silver;** (h), (i) **bronze; found at** (a) **Plumstead,** (b) **Mitcham Common,** (c) **Lewisham,**
(d) **Barnet,** (e) **Victoria Park,** (f) **Verulamium,** (g) **Chiswick,** (h) **Barnes,** (i) **Shepperton**

the tribe, or within the area under its political dominance.

The first wave of Belgic immigrants is marked by the distribution of a type of gold coin which had a recognizable head with long curly hair, and a just recognizable horse and chariot (*fig. 25a*). These seem to have originated in the Somme Valley of northern France, and were probably brought to Britain by Belgic people who were displaced from that region by invaders from the Rhineland between 150 and 100 B.C. They seem to have reached the Lower Thames by way of Kent, and penetrated north of the Thames into Hertfordshire, and also by way of Essex into East Anglia.

The next Belgic immigration, as indicated by the distribution of its coins, affected the London area much more directly, since the invaders seem to have travelled up the Thames Valley, and to have taken possession of part of what is now Greater London, including the long favoured district upstream of Central London. The coins of these people are curious, in that the head on the one side was always deliberately defaced on the die, and sometimes the chariot on the other side received the same treatment (*fig. 25b*). It seems likely that this had some political meaning, and that these settlers are a portion of a tribe who broke away from the

41

rest of their people, and demonstrated their independence by defacing the tribal coinage. These coins are called *Gallo-Belgic B* to distinguish them from the first coins introduced, which are called *Gallo-Belgic A*. The type before defacement was not quite the same as that of the Gallo-Belgic A coins, and may have come from a more northerly part of Gaul. Both of these invasions probably took place well before 100 B.C. A third incursion seems to have arrived in Kent at about that date, bringing with it a type of gold coin. *Gallo-Belgic C*, in which the process of disintegration of the head on one side and the chariot on the other had been carried further, so that both were now hardly recognizable (*fig. 25c*). It is this type that was soon being copied on the first coins produced in Britain. Gallo-Belgic C coins only reached the south-eastern part of the London region, most of which was presumably still controlled by the Gallo-Belgic B people.

There was a steady reduction of the weight of Gallo-Belgic and British gold coins as time went by, and the distribution of new types of light weight seems to indicate two later incursions from Gaul, each with its own distinctive coins, *Gallo-Belgic D* and *E*. The people who brought these were probably refugees from Caesar's conquests of Gaul in 59-51 B.C. They reached the London region through Kent, and a number of the Gallo-Belgic E coins, which are plain on one side, have been found there (*fig. 25d*).

THE INVASION OF JULIUS CAESAR

At about this time a powerful Belgic chieftain, Cassivellaunus, was ruling to the north of the Thames, which seems now to have been regarded more as a tribal frontier than a convenient means of travel. He was almost certainly king of the Catuvellauni, a tribe of Hertfordshire, whose boundary extended to the Thames; and he evidently had a great reputation as a war-leader, since he was chosen to take command when the tribes of south-eastern Britain briefly united against Julius Caesar in the Roman expedition of 54 B.C. After giving the Romans some trouble at first by attacking with chariots, which the tribes in Gaul no longer used, and which were therefore unfamiliar to the Romans, he was defeated in Kent and withdrew to the north of the Thames. The Romans succeeded in crossing, in the face of opposition, at a difficult ford, which had been defended by sharp stakes fixed on the bank and in the river-bed. This ford, which Caesar believed to be the only one, must have been the first

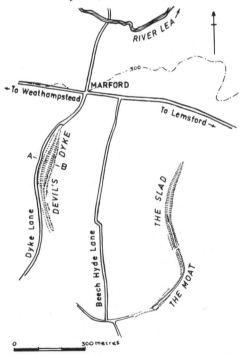

Fig. 26 Plan showing position of Belgic fortress at Wheathampstead

42

crossing-place he reached, and it is more likely to have been in what is now Central London than farther upstream at Brentford, which is often claimed to be the site of the crossing. We are told that the infantry were up to their necks in water, and there is reason to believe that the Brentford crossing was much easier than this. (See p. 34). While Caesar was trying to make his way into the interior, harassed by Catuvellaunian guerillas, who knew the paths through the woods, he was contacted by envoys from the Trinovantes of Essex, who surrendered, and then supplied the Romans with grain—another indication that they were probably not operating very far up the river. Other tribes, named the Cenimagni, Segontiaci, Ancalites, Bibroci and Cassi then surrendered. Some of these must have been local people of the London region, probably under the domination of the Catuvellauni. They were able to show Caesar the way to the woodland stronghold of Cassivellaunus, strongly fortified and protected by forests and marshes.

WHEATHAMPTEAD BELGIC STRONGHOLD

Belgic strongholds of this kind were not hill-forts, but were densely wooded places fortified by a rampart and ditch. A site in Catuvellaunian territory that seems to fit Caesar's description is to be found near Wheathampstead, just to the south of a ford over the River Lea. On its north side it would have been protected by the marshes of the Lea Valley; on the west by a huge ditch with a bank on each side, 40 ft deep and 130 ft wide, called the Devil's Dyke; and on the east by a similar ditch called the Slad (*figs. 26 and 27*). The enclosed area, which is on boulder-clay and would have been naturally wooded, has been estimated to be nearly a hundred acres. A great boundary ditch evidently associated with these defences is Beech Bottom Dyke, which runs in a south-westerly direction towards the Ver. It is quite possible that Wheathampstead was the fortress which Caesar tells us he successfully attacked on two sides, driving out the warriors of Cassivellaunus by another. After the failure of a British attack on the Roman naval camp in Kent, Cassivellaunus sued for peace and surrendered hostages, whom Caesar took back with him to Gaul.

COMMIUS AND THE ATREBATES

The go-between in these negotiations was a Belgic chieftain named Commius, at this time friendly towards the Romans. Later, however, he became one of the leaders of Gaulish resistance to Caesar, and he eventually fled to Britain, where part of his tribe, the Atrebates, had settled in what is now Berkshire, northern and eastern Hampshire, and western Sussex. Commius founded here a great rival dynasty to that of Cassivellaunus. His name, COMMIOS, is the first to be inscribed on any British

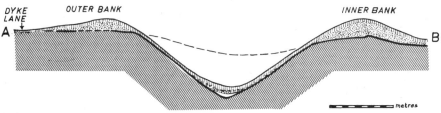

Fig. 27 Section through Devil's Dyke, Wheathampstead

coin—in the period from about 35 to 30 B.C., when he had already been a ruling chieftain for a quarter of a century. His sons, Tincommius, Eppillus and Verica, who ruled in succession after him, all proudly call themselves COM F—short for COMMII FILIUS, (son of Commius)—on their coins. In the London region none of these coins are found north of the Thames, which evidently here formed the tribal boundary, and in the Thames Valley they do not occur east of Kingston, where a gold coin of Tincommius was found. It is only the south-western part of our region, therefore, that formed part of the kingdom of the Atrebates, and even here, as we shall see, there were encroachments from the Catuvellauni.

THE CATUVELLAUNI

Cassivellaunus did not put his name on his coins, and it is by no means certain which type of uninscribed coin he issued. The first king of the Catuvellauni whose name appeared on coins is Tasciovanus, who probably reigned from about 20 B.C., and may have been a grandson of Cassivellaunus (*fig. 25e*). On his later coins the mint name VER for *Verulamium* appears (*fig. 25f*)—in one instance in full as VER-VLAMIO. The tribal capital lay to the south-west of the later (Roman) city, partly in Prae Wood, but extending far to the south-east beyond it. The site is on a plateau west of the valley of the river Ver, and near a ford in the river. It was bounded to the north and north-east by a ditch and palisade, and was divided by another palisade, which perhaps separated an inhabited area to the north-west from a cattle-pound to the south-east. Within an angle of the defences to the north was a small enclosure, possibly also used for cattle. Cart-ruts were found to the south of its southern entrance, towards which they were pointing. Excavations showed that the original defences of Belgic Verulamium were slight, but that they had been strengthened in the north-western section by adding another ditch and palisade, not earlier than about A.D. 25-50, and in all probability at the time of the Roman invasion of A.D. 43.

TRIBAL WARS AND CONQUESTS

There was trouble between the Catuvellauni and their neighbours to the east, the Trinovantes, in the time of Caesar. This evidently continued into the reign of Tasciovanus, when a king named Addedomaros ruled the Trinovantes. Judging from the distribution of his coins, he was able to extend his rule at times into the territory of the Catuvellauni. One of his coins was found at Chiswick (*fig. 25g*), and others have been found in Buckinghamshire, as well as farther up the Thames Valley. Tasciovanus, on the other hand, must at one time have gained control of Camulodunum (Colchester), the tribal capital of the Trinovantes, since one of his coins has an abbreviation of the name of that mint. He must also have ruled over parts of north and west Kent, especially west of the Medway, where a number of his coins have been found.

Dubnovellaunus, a king of Kent, for a time ruled territory on both sides of the Thames Estuary, but seems to have lost control in Kent and was eventually driven out. Eppillus, one of the sons of Commius, then seems to have made himself king of East Kent, after being ousted from the rule of the Atrebates, probably by his brother Verica.

A greater ruler then succeeded in establishing his empire over three of the

Fig. 28 Belgic wheel-made pottery from Wheathampstead, 1st century B.C.

major tribes of S.E. Britain, as well as many lesser ones. Cunobelinus, the son of Tasciovanus, succeeded his father as king of the Catuvellauni, and extended his power over both the Trinovantes and the Cantii, making Camulodunum his capital and mint (*fig. 25h*). He even succeeded in gaining some control over part of the Atrebates, where his brother Epaticcus was made king, and coins with the corn-ear of the Catuvellaunian dynasty now circulated in the kingdom of the Atrebates, among those with the rival badge of the vine-leaf, emblem of the family of Commius.

THE BELGIC WAY OF LIFE

In addition to their organizing ability, which seems almost to foreshadow that of the Romans themselves, the Belgae made important contributions to technological progress in Britain. Due to their partly Germanic origin, they were at home in the woodlands where, as we have seen, they preferred to build their fortresses. They were skilled in clearing the heavy clay soils of the valleys, which earlier settlers had avoided, and which were now exploited for the first time. They also developed some crafts on an industrial scale. Their blacksmiths were particularly skilful, and made complex wrought-iron fire-dogs and slave-chains; their potters introduced the use of the wheel, and turned into an industry what had previously been a household craft (*fig. 28*). There was already a long-standing tradition of fine bronze-work in Britain, but this received a great stimulus from the patronage of the Belgic chiefs, and some of the finest examples of late Celtic art were produced in south-eastern Britain during the period of Belgic domination. As in earlier times, a number of these found their way into the Thames, by accident or, more probably, as votive offerings (*fig. 29*).

The Belgae cremated their dead, and burials rich in grave goods have been found at Welwyn, Welwyn Garden City and Hertford Heath, evidently belonging to the Catuvellaunian aristocracy, and dating

Fig. 29 Bronze shield from Thames at Battersea, early 1st century A.D.

from about 50 to 10 B.C. These contained amphorae imported as containers of wine from the Mediterranean, the characteristic wheel-made Belgic jars with pedestal bases, and bronze vessels from Italy. The grave from Welwyn Garden City and one of those from Welwyn also contained fine imported Roman silver cups of the later part of the 1st century B.C. (*fig. 30a*). Purely Celtic, however, are three little cast bronze faces with moustaches (*fig. 30b*) and wrought-iron fire-dogs with terminals in the form of horned animal heads from the Welwyn graves. Most interesting of all, perhaps, is a set of twenty-four glass pieces for some kind of board game, found with the Welwyn Garden City burial.

There is considerable evidence of increased Continental trade with the Belgic chieftains of S.E. Britain, especially after about 10 B.C. when a great deal of Italian and South Gaulish fine pottery was imported. In these circumstances it might be expected that the Thames would again come to the fore as the gateway of Britain. This does not seem to have been the case, however, and theories of a pre-Roman Thames-side trading station have never been confirmed by archaeological evidence. The reason seems to be that the Thames was now a political frontier, too exposed to attack from the rival Atrebates to provide a safe site for an important settlement of the Catuvellauni. The capture of Camulodunum provided ready access to trade with southern Europe, and a safe site for the tribal capital. If Cunobelinus had lived long enough after consolidating his power on both sides of the river, he might well have felt the need for a more central capital, and a pre-Roman London might have developed. Camulodunum, however, was conveniently placed for contact with his Belgic kinsmen of east Kent, and he had much less in common with the tribes of west

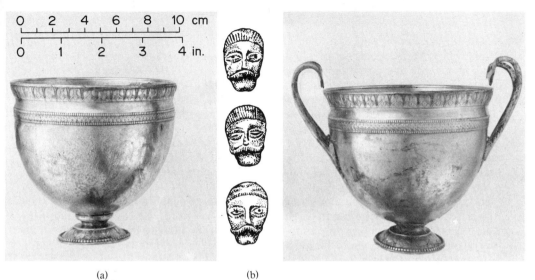

(a) (b)

Fig. 30 Finds at Welwyn associated with Belgic cremation burials
(a) silver cups imported from Italy, (b) cast bronze ornaments

Kent, although they had been dominated by the Catuvellauni since the time of Tasciovanus.

The people west of the Medway were non-Belgic, and their pottery shows their relationship to the mixed population of the Sussex Weald, in whom Iron Age A and B traditions were mingled. Bowls with small foot-rings of Iron Age B origin found both in the Darenth Valley and in Surrey can be traced back into the Weald and ultimately to the South Downs. Later immigrants from the Continent, with a non-Belgic B culture ('*South-eastern B*'). also found their way from the Sussex coast into west Kent and across the Thames, introducing a type of globular bowl with indented base, decorated with impressed circles and 'eyebrow'-like curved grooves. These were sometimes used as cremation urns. In the same period just before the Roman conquest, but continuing in use to a later date, were large storage pots in which there was a curious revival of the Iron Age A and Bronze Age practice of decorating with rows of finger-tip impressions or slashes ('Patch Grove' type). They are common in the Darenth Valley, but also extend farther west, and likewise seem to reflect a Sussex fashion of this time. Neckless jars with thickened rims (bead-rims), called the *Charlton* type, after a fortified site above the Thames near Woolwich, are even more common, with a wide distribution south of the Thames, westward from the Medway Valley. They have been found in east Kent, but are not characteristic of the Belgic sites north of the Thames.

A non-Belgic feature of a different kind that is characteristic of the Thames Valley during this period, especially in the London area, is a very barbarous coinage of bronze

47

rich in tin. These coins were cast in moulds, and have crude representations of a human head on one side and a butting bull on the other (*fig. 25i*). This coinage developed in Kent, copying the cast coins of northern Gaul, which were derived by way of central Gaul from bronze coins of Marseilles. It is quite different in style from the Belgic gold and silver coinage and follows a different tradition. Such coins are found throughout north Kent, in the Thames Valley, the eastern counties, and on the Sussex coast, with a scattering farther west in Wessex. There is a distinct concentration in the western part of London, where hoards have been found in St James's Park, Hammersmith, Brentford, Shepperton and Gunnersbury, probably brought by refugees from Kent at the time of Julius Caesar's invasion. They seem to have been used throughout the century immediately before the Roman conquest, since worn examples were found in the Snettisham hoard of about 25 B.C., while others have been excavated from early Roman occupation levels, as at Lullingstone.

All this suggests that there was a very mixed, but mainly non-Belgic population in the London area at this time. Included in it, no doubt, were some of the obscure tribes mentioned by Caesar. Although nominally under Catuvellaunian rule, they owed their Belgic overlord no loyalty, and were probably no more to be trusted than in the time of Cassivellaunus. In these circumstances, Cunobelinus, like his predecessors, saw no advantage in establishing his headquarters on the exposed bank of the Thames. London's day was yet to come.

7 Under Roman Rule

The Roman invasion of A.D. 43 almost at once gave birth to London, and very soon provided the conditions under which the infant city grew and flourished. The first London Bridge was established by the Roman army as an essential part of the plan for the pacification of Britain, which depended on good communications. The position chosen was as near the river mouth as possible, although it had to be just upstream of the part then affected by the tides, where the mud flats became a wide lake at high tide. This gave the shortest journey between the invasion ports of Kent and the Belgic capital at Camulodunum, where the Emperor Claudius had decided to establish the capital of the new Roman province. The chosen crossing-place was from a sandy heath a few feet higher than the low-lying country on either side, and protected on the east side by a stream or creek. Opposite, on the far side of the river, was a steep bank and considerably higher ground, only lightly wooded. A little way upstream this was broken by the valley of another tributary which would give similar protection to the northern end of the crossing. Here Aulus Plautius built his

48

bridge, very near the site of the present London Bridge, perhaps even before the arrival of Claudius in the late summer of A.D. 43. We have evidence of early military activity near Aldgate, and both ends of the bridge must have been defended. London really began, therefore, with the military occupation of Cornhill as a bridge-head in an early phase of the Conquest.

THE ROMAN ROADS

The laying out of the main Roman roads soon followed, since they were needed for the rapid movement of troops and supplies. In south-eastern Britain, the roads on both sides of the river had to come to the bridge, so that it became an important centre of communications—and this is what London has been ever since. It was not only a centre for travel by land, however; it could also be reached by water. Ships from the Continent could sail up the Thames to the bridge, and there unload goods and men for distribution along the new roads wherever they were needed. From the beginning, therefore, London was a port, as indeed it has remained to this day.

The roads then laid out have also continued in use as important highways for most of their lengths, although they have been re-made many times, and the modern tarmac is quite different from the rammed gravel of the Romans. This also gave a smooth surface, however, when mud had set hard in the crevices between the pebbles, and it was very firm and strong. The Romans had to use local material, which they needed in great quantities. In the London region they naturally turned to the terraces of ancient river gravel, which had already served men well for thousands of years. Often, a foundation of large stones was laid for better drainage, and sometimes

the surface was raised on an embankment. It was usually cambered for drainage into side-ditches. The gravel metalling was often quite thin, but repairs were made by laying a new surface over the old, and when this process was repeated many times a great thickness could be built up.

In this activity the Roman engineers were true pioneers, who surveyed these alignments for the first time, in country that was often densely wooded. They worked with military precision in straight lines, from one sighting point to the next, but were always ready to deflect to a new alignment when the nature of the ground made it advisable, returning to the more direct course as soon as the difficulty was past. It says much for their skill that the routes they chose could not, in many stretches, be improved by their successors.

For example, the Roman road later called Watling Street, which linked the landing-place and supply base of Aulus Plautius at Richborough to his bridge over the Thames, is now the A207 between Greenwich Park and Dartford, and the A2 for a considerable part of the way between Dartford and Rochester. The Roman road from Londinium to Camulodunum is overlaid by the A118 for long stretches eastward from Romford Road to Romford, by Colchester Road and London Road between Gidea Park and Brentwood, and by the A12 in its approach to Chelmsford (*Caesaromagus*). Ermine Street, the Roman road to the north, underlies the A10 from Bishopsgate to Edmonton, where it leaves the modern highway. The Roman road from Newgate to Silchester (*Calleva*) is followed by Oxford Street and Bayswater Road, and then fairly closely by the A40 and A402 to Acton. Farther west the A315 continues the line, which becomes the A30 from East Bedfont to Staines. Watling Street, the Roman road to Verulamium, left this road at Marble Arch on the line of what is now Edgware Road, and the A5 barely departs from it all the way to St Albans. Stane Street, the Roman road from London Bridge to Chichester (*Regnum*) lies under or fairly close to the modern A3 and A24 roads through South London to Merton, and after a break is again followed by the A24 through Cheam.

The archaeologist, of course, is more interested in the places where the modern road has departed from the ancient line, for here it is sometimes possible to find the Roman road by excavation. Unfortunately, in our region, due to the intensive use of land since Roman times, there are seldom any traces on the surface that are visible to the non-expert—and even the expert often finds that he was mistaken when there is an opportunity to excavate! This is a fascinating field for study, which cannot be discussed in detail here. The reader is referred to I.D. Margary's *Roman Roads in Britain* (revised edition, 1967) and for further reference to my chapters on Roman roads in Greater London in *Roman London* (1969).

FORTS

Several forts and fortlets probably belong to the period of conquest and pacification, and there are no doubt more to be discovered. One was at Chelmsford, half-way to Camulodunum; and a small fort overlooking the Thames estuary at Orsett, Essex, had its ditches recut five times in the mid-1st century. A fortlet observed on air photographs west of Hadleigh may be of the invasion period or later. A V-shaped military ditch at Aldgate, however, containing a Roman sword-grip in its fill, is an early feature, and must have been dug by the army of Aulus Plautius.

ROMAN VERULAMIUM

When the road to the north-west was laid out, a small fort, with a timber-revetted bank and a wooden watch-tower at one corner, was built on its line, in the neighbourhood of the tribal capital of the Catuvellauni at Verulamium. Here, in spite of the move of the court of Cunobelinus to Camulodunum, a large settlement still flourished, and had spread from its woodland stronghold into the valley. It was probably the task of the small Roman garrison to supervise the layout and building of the new town that now appeared. This was intended to transform the natives into civilized townspeople in the Roman fashion. A regular system of streets intersecting at right-angles was laid out, dividing the new town into square blocks or *insulae*. Barrack-like wooden shops were built, probably by the Roman soldiers, facing the new road of Watling Street. They were in a continuous row with a verandah in front, giving some protection to the wide open entrances, which could be closed by hinged shutters when the shop was shut. A second room lay behind. One shop contained many fragments of amphorae or wine-jars, and was probably a wine shop; in another, furniture was probably made, since carpenters' tools were found there; a third had a working area behind, where there was a hearth or oven, apparently used for bronze-working, since crucibles, figurines and filed fragments of bronze were found nearby. These shops had foundations of oak beams laid in trenches, and walls of wattle and daub supported by vertical posts. A V-shaped ditch was dug as part of the defences of the new town, but before these were finished, disaster came, and the wooden buildings were completely destroyed by fire.

Londinium and Verulamium were the

only important towns founded by the Romans in the London region, and Verulamium was given the constitution of a *municipium*, or second-class town, which meant that its citizens had certain well-defined rights, greater than those of an ordinary tribal capital, which was called a *civitas*. The new Roman town at Camulodunum was of even higher status as a *colonia*, or first-class town, but its settlers were not conquered Britons but retired soldiers, who were Roman citizens, with the same prestige and legal rights as those born free in Rome itself. Curiously, the status of Londinium does not seem to have been decided at first, perhaps because it was under the direct rule of the Roman government, and we know only that seventeen years after its foundation it was not a *colonia*.

POSTING-STATIONS

Other much smaller settlements grew up at suitable places along the Roman roads. Posting stations were established at regular intervals along them, to provide resting places and changes of horses for messengers and other travelling officials. The government rest-house attracted tradesmen and other settlers, and markets for the produce of the surrounding countryside developed. In suitable places local industries also sprang up, and the posting station became a small town or village. The origin of such settlements is shown by their siting at fairly regular distances along the main Roman roads.

Nine miles from Verulamium and twelve from Londinium, the posting station was placed on Brockley Hill, where the road changed direction. We know from the *Antonine Itinerary*, an official road-book of about A.D. 200, that it was called *Sulloniacae*. Here the local clay was suitable for making pottery, and a

flourishing industry soon developed, producing buff-coloured kitchen-ware for the markets of Londinium and Verulamium, and even farther afield. Kilns have been found here during rescue excavations of recent years, together with great quantities of broken pottery.

Also 12 miles from Londinium, but on the opposite side of the river, a prosperous Roman settlement seems to have developed at Ewell, on Stane Street, the road to Chichester. We do not know very much about it, but Roman luxury goods have been found there, as well as many Roman pottery fragments. From its position, it is likely to have been the site of the first posting station out of Londinium.

On Watling Street, the road to Richborough and Dover, the Antonine Itinerary tells us that the first posting station was *Noviomagus*, 10 miles from Londinium. This would put it at Welling, where there are only slight indications of Roman occupation, and as there are other errors in the distances given on this road, it is likely that *Noviomagus* was actually at Crayford, 3 miles farther on, where there was a considerable Roman settlement. This road crossed the Medway at Rochester, called *Durobrivae* in the Itinerary, and here there was another posting stage and settlement. An intermediate station, called *Vagniacae*, was almost certainly at Springhead, where a sacred spring became the site of an important group of temples.

On the road to Camulodunum there was a posting station at *Durolitum*, perhaps at Romford, where no definite evidence of Roman occupation has yet been found; and a more important settlement with the high-sounding title of *Caesaromagus*, developed on the site of the early fort at Chelmsford.

A small town grew up around the posting station at Staines, on the road to Silchester and the west, where the river was evidently crossed by more than one bridge, since the settlement was called *Pontes*—'The Bridges'. Traces of Roman wattle and daub buildings, wells, a kiln, and two parallel gravel roads have recently been found there. One of these, just beside the present High Street, was of a very early date, and may well have been the first road to Silchester. It was overlaid by a burnt layer, indicating that here, as at Verulamium, disaster came soon after the founding of the settlement.

BOUDICCA'S REVOLT

It also came to Londinium, where a bright red layer of burnt clay, from the walls of wattle and daub houses destroyed by fire, has often been seen in excavations just above the original natural ground level, now deeply buried beneath the man-made accumulations of nearly two thousand years. It contains and covers pottery, and occasionally coins, of the mid-1st century, and there is little doubt of its exact date and origin, either here or at Verulamium. For it is a fact of history that both these cities went up in flames in A.D. 60, when a great British revolt almost succeeded in destroying Roman rule in this country. It was led by Boudicca, Queen of the Iceni of East Anglia, provoked beyond endurance by the insults and greed of the agents of the Procurator, the high Roman official who was responsible to the Emperor for the financial affairs of Britain. This followed the death of her husband, who had vainly tried to preserve some of his wealth for his family by bequeathing part of it to the Emperor. Hitherto the Iceni had remained a client kingdom, bound by treaty to the Romans, but not directly ruled by them. The brutality which sparked off the revolt took place while the kingdom was being taken over to become part of the Roman Province.

The Iceni were joined by their neighbours to the south, the Trinovantes of Essex, who resented the loss of their tribal lands to the arrogant Roman colonists settled at Camulodunum. The expensive state cult of Emperor worship, established there as a focus of loyalty, also roused their anger. Camulodunum therefore became the first target of the rebels, and it offered little resistance. Here the pattern of massacre and burning was first set, and part of the Ninth Legion, which attempted a relief, was ambushed with heavy losses. The Procurator himself escaped by ship, probably from London, which may already have been his headquarters.

The main part of the Roman army was campaigning in Anglesey under the military Governor, Suetonius Paulinus. When the news reached him, his first thought was to save London, which he managed to reach with his cavalry before the rebels. He realized that he had insufficient troops to defend the town, and so he was forced to abandon both Londinium and Verulamium, taking with him all who could march and were willing to leave their homes. The two cities were burnt by the rebels, and the remaining inhabitants slaughtered. Altogether, Tacitus tells us, 70,000 perished in Camulodunum, Londinium and Verulamium. In the stream-bed of the London Walbrook, many human skulls have been found, bearing witness to an ancient massacre. We have no proof of its date, but it is by no means unlikely that decapitated heads were thrown into the stream on this occasion, perhaps in some barbarous tribal rite.

After rejoining his force from Anglesey, Suetonius met Boudicca's horde in battle, somewhere near the line of Watling Street, and Roman discipline prevailed over

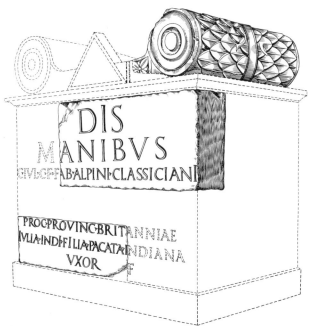

Fig. 31 Tombstone of Classicianus, reconstructed from fragments found on Tower Hill

immensely superior numbers. The victory was a crushing one, and Boudicca poisoned herself. There followed a ruthless punishment of the rebel tribes, in which their territory was laid waste. One Roman disapproved of this, and had the courage to oppose it. The new Procurator, C. Julius Alpinus Classicianus, exercised his right of direct appeal to the Emperor, pointing out the ill effects of this destruction on the economy of Britain. This argument had its effect, and after an official enquiry Suetonius Paulinus was replaced by a new Governor.

THE TOMBSTONE OF CLASSICIANUS

Classicianus died in office and was buried in London, where two portions of the inscription from his tombstone were found, re-used as building material in a bastion of the city wall on Tower Hill (*fig. 31*). The first portion, with the Procurator's name, was found in 1852, and correctly identified by the Victorian antiquary, Charles Roach Smith. Later scholars could not believe that a casual archaeological find really contained a name from the pages of Tacitus; but the discovery of the second portion in 1935 clinched the matter, for there was the official title of Classicianus— PROC(VRATOR) PROVINC(IAE) BRIT- (ANNIAE). The reconstructed tombstone, now in the British Museum, bears witness to the fact that, soon after A.D. 61, Londinium was already the headquarters of the financial administration of the province. Also in the British Museum is a wooden writing tablet from the Walbrook, branded with the official stamp of the Procurator's office, and evidently used by one of his clerks.

As the re-building of Londinium proceeded, it seems to have taken over more of the former functions of Camulodunum as the administrative capital. A great public building stood in the heart of the city where the northern part of Gracechurch Street now lies. Beside it bakers' ovens were built, perhaps to prepare food for its staff. All this was to be swept away before the end of the 1st century to make room for a large basilica and forum. The basilica, which combined the functions of town hall and court of justice, was more than 500 ft long, almost twice the length of any other basilica in Britain. Adjoining it to the south was the forum, with buildings on three sides forming with the basilica a great square enclosure. This was the business and civic centre of Londinium. The basilica would have contained the *curia,* or senate-house, and the building of it indicates that London

had received local self-government. Its status as a town must now have been defined, but we do not know what it was.

Verulamium was also provided with a basilica (partly underlying St Michael's Church) and with a forum extending to the south of the basilica. In this case the building can be exactly dated by fragments of an inscription from the entrance (*fig. 32*). Ingeniously reconstructed by experts, it tells us that the basilica dates from the Governorship of Agricola, the father-in-law of Tacitus, and Governor of Britain from A.D. 78 to 84. Other details indicate that the precise date was 79, the very year that, according to Tacitus, Agricola launched an ambitious policy of education and romanization in Britain, pressing forward the construction of temples, forums and town-houses. Probably the London basilica and forum were planned as part of the same programme, but the existence of an important public building on the site may

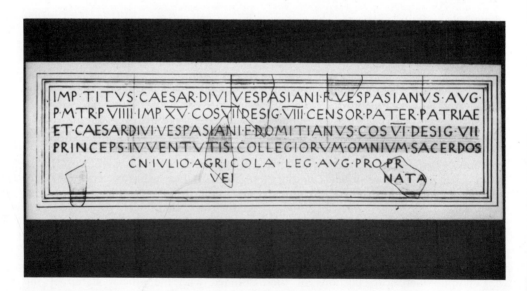

Fig. 32 Reconstructed inscription from the basilica at Verulamium

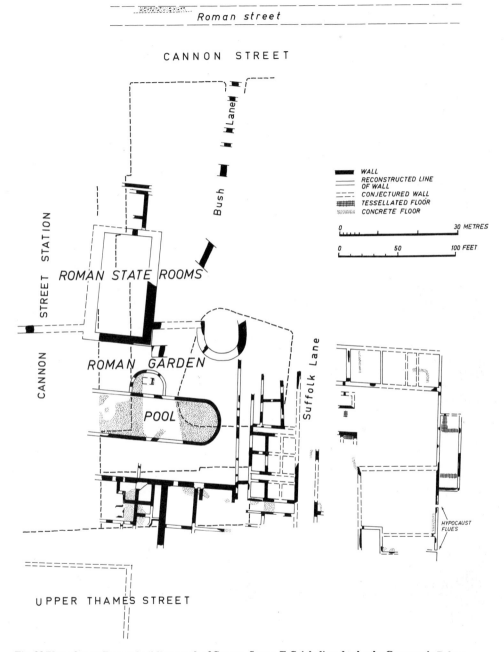

Fig. 33 Plan of great Roman building south of Cannon Street, E.C.4, believed to be the Governor's Palace

55

have delayed the completion of the London forum for a few years.

Tacitus also tells us that the Britons were encouraged to enjoy the pleasures of civilization, including those provided by the public baths. It is not surprising, therefore, that about this time a large bathing establishment was built in Londinium. The gravel slope above the Thames in Upper built between A.D. 80 and 90. It underlies Cannon Street Station and extended at least 340 ft to the east of it. It contained large halls, massively built, and suites of smaller rooms, possibly offices. In a central court was a great ornamental pool (*fig. 33*). It was clearly an official palace, and is likely to have been the residence of the Governor himself.

Fig. 34 South-west corner of Roman fort, Noble Street, E.C.2

Thames Street was terraced, and the usual hot, warm and cold rooms were built into the hillside, with a cold plunge bath as the final stage after passing through what would now be called a Turkish bath.

Agricola or his successor was also probably responsible for a very much larger public building, similarly set into the hillside above the Thames, and apparently

THE FORT OF LONDINIUM

The building of a stone fort of about 12 acres to the north-west of the city, early in the 2nd century, may reflect London's status. Soldiers were needed in the capital as sentries and escorts; but as the Romans ruled with a military government, they were also needed for many official duties that would today be carried out by civil servants. The main purpose of the fort may have been as a barracks for these troops, rather than as a defence for London. It was, however, provided with all the regular defensive structures; external ditch, internal bank, corner and intermediate turrets, no doubt in conformity with army regulations (*fig.34*).

LONDINIUM AND VERULAMIUM IN THE 2ND CENTURY

Londinium seems to have attained its full extended much farther than did that of the Boudiccan fire, indicating the growth of the city in the meantime. It covered an area of at least 65 acres.

Verulamium also had its second fire, after about A.D. 155, and was rebuilt with much more substantial private houses, constructed partly in flint and mortar. In spite of this disaster, the 2nd century seems to have been a period of prosperity for Verulamium. Many houses had fine mosaic floors and elaborate frescoes. About the middle of the 2nd century, also, a fine

Fig. 35 Roman theatre at Verulamium as excavated in 1933, from N.W.

splendour by about the middle of the 2nd century, perhaps as a sequel to Hadrian's visit in A.D. 122. The fort, and probably also the forum, had been completed, and a second bath suite had been added to the public baths. A disastrous fire, probably in this case accidental, destroyed the greater part of the city about A.D. 130, but was only a temporary setback. The fire debris theatre was built, with a circular central space that could be used either as the orchestra of a theatre or as the arena of an amphitheatre. Adjoining it was a small stage, and stone-revetted earth banks for tiers of wooden seats formed three-quarters of a circle around it (*fig. 35*). It could have accommodated 5000-6000 people.

Near the theatre on Watling Street was a

triumphal arch, one of three found in Verulamium, all of which stood on Watling Street. The other two were placed close to the positions where this main street passed through the earlier defences, and may have been built to commemorate the later enlargement of the town's boundaries.

TEMPLES

Adjoining the theatre to the south-west was a square temple within an oblong enclosure. It was built in the late 1st century, and continued in use all through the Roman period. It is quite likely that the theatre had some connection with this temple, and was used in religious festivals as well as for entertainment. Another temple was built early in the 2nd century on a triangular site where Watling Street crossed the regular street-grid.

In Londinium the only known temple is of a different type, with nave, side aisles and a raised sanctuary within an apse, in plan very much like a Christian church. It was built on the east bank of the Walbrook, about the middle of the 3rd century, for the rites of Mithras, which were performed by initiates in secrecy. About A.D. 300 or a little later, some danger, probably from Christian hostility, led to marble sculptures being buried, including the head of Mithras. They were never recovered, but the temple continued to be used, and was still pagan in its final phase, when a marble group of Bacchus, the wine-god, with his usual companions, stood in the temple.

CITY WALLS

Within a few years of A.D. 200, Londinium was provided with a great stone wall, more than 2 miles long, built of Kentish ragstone, quarried near Maidstone and brought to London by barge. The wall is dated by pottery and coins found in earlier deposits, and by the debris thrown away by a coin-forger about A.D. 220 into one of its turrets, where quite a lot of rubbish had already accumulated. A Roman barge that had been fitted with its mast in the 2nd century—on the evidence of a worn coin of A.D. 88-9, put in the mast-step for luck on that occasion—was found wrecked with its

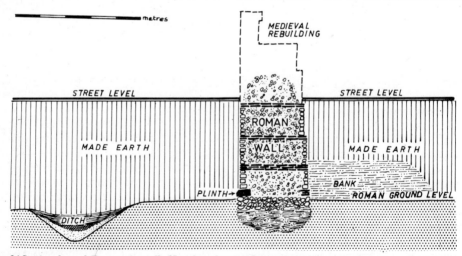

Fig. 36 Section through Roman city wall of London, showing the portion that usually survives

cargo of ragstone near Blackfriars Bridge. It seems to have been broken up on the river bed during the 3rd century, so it is quite probable that it was wrecked while carrying stone for the city wall. The vessel was large, and it has been roughly estimated that it could have carried 900 cubic ft of stone. Even so, not less than thirteen hundred similar barge-loads would have been needed for the wall. Much more would have been required if the builders had not made use of two walls of the fort built some 80 years earlier. The new city wall was built to meet the north-east and south-west corners of the fort, so that the north and west walls of the latter now became part of the city wall. They were, however, much thinner than the new wall, and were therefore brought to the required strength by the addition of a thickening on the inside.

The faces of the city wall were built of ragstone blocks squared by masons and laid in regular courses like bricks. At least a million of these would have been needed. The core of the wall, however, is composed of rubble concrete—irregular lumps of ragstone set in mortar. Except in the composite wall on the north and west sides of the fort, double or triple courses of building tiles run right through the wall at regular intervals. Just above Roman ground-level, however, a triple course of these tiles forms a facing only on the inside of the wall. At the corresponding level on the outside is a plinth of large blocks of sandstone, also from Kent. A ditch was dug outside the wall, and the material from this and from the foundation trench was thrown up against the inside of the wall to form a bank (*fig. 36*).

The most likely occasion for such a great effort in defence of Londinium seems to be the period between 193 and 196, when Clodius Albinus, the Governor of Britain, was preparing for war with Septimius Severus, in his unsuccessful bid for the Empire. He knew that he would have to take all the available troops to the Continent, leaving the towns of Britain in danger. Many of them were provided with earth ramparts in the later 2nd century—a task for unskilled labour—but for the capital a greater effort seems to have been made.

The story of Verulamium's defences is more complex. The smaller town of the late 1st century had been defended by a ditch, which had been filled in early in the 2nd century. After the town had grown to its fullest extent, an earth rampart and ditch were constructed but perhaps not completed. A new and slightly smaller circuit was then defended by a masonry wall as massive as that of Londinium, but built mainly of flint. Here also double and triple tile courses run through the wall at regular intervals, and there is an internal bank. The external ditch was doubled on the west side. Two of the gates were built before the masonry wall, probably for the earlier earthwork defence, but the Silchester gate was built at the same time as the wall and, on the evidence of a small coin hoard found concealed in it, was in existence before A.D. 250. The wall of Verulamium was therefore probably built soon after that of Londinium, early in the 3rd century. Town defences had evidently proved their value in the maintenance of law and order, and continued to be improved and extended by Severus and his successors.

INDUSTRIES

Crafts as well as trade flourished in the Roman towns. In later times, as there had been before the destruction of A.D. 60, there were bronze-workers in Verulamium, and in Londinium a gold-smith was at work on the hillside above the Thames about

Fig. 37 Internal face of Roman city wall of London, Wakefield Gardens, Tower Hill

A.D. 80. It is quite likely that many small personal ornaments such as brooches were made in these two towns. Traces of actual business correspondence deciphered on a wooden writing-tablet from Londinium suggest that there was a local ship-building industry. There was also a state brickworks making tiles for public buildings, and using the stamps PP.BR. or P.PR.BR., often with the addition of LON. for *Londinii*—'at London'. The meaning of the first P. is doubtful, but PR. BR. must be an abbreviation for PROVINCIAE BRITANNIAE—'of the Province of Britain'. Leather-working was certainly carried on in the neighbourhood of the Walbrook, where fragments of cut leather have been found; and pottery was made in the western part of the city. Service trades for the townspeople included milling and baking, and in Londinium the upper stone of a donkey-mill was found near the Walbrook. A well-to-do townsman of Verulamium provided another essential service, no doubt for profit, by making part of his large house into a public lavatory.

The countryside must have been concerned mainly with the production of food—agriculture, market-gardening, stock-breeding and dairy-farming, although some industry developed where there were suitable resources and facilities for transport. The principal raw materials were clay and brick-earth for potting and the manufacture of tiles. The pottery kilns in the settlements that grew up round the posting-stations of *Sulloniacae* (Brockley Hill) and *Pontes* (Staines) have already been mentioned. There were also flourishing pottery industries in the latter part of the 1st and early 2nd century in Highgate Wood, North London, and on the low-lying lands of North Kent near Upchurch, now marshes but then dry ground. Tiles were produced on Ashtead Common, from the 1st century A.D., on a site linked with Stane Street by a well-made road.

Salt was an important product of the Thames Estuary, as it had been in the pre-Roman Iron Age. Sites used for its extraction are indicated by fragments of burnt clay from evaporating furnaces, producing deposits sometimes called 'Red Hills'. They are associated with Roman pottery at Cooling, North Kent, and on Canvey Island, Essex, as well as on the marshes of the river Crouch in Essex.

VILLAS

The requirements of the new towns and of Roman officialdom encouraged the development of agriculture, and a number of villas (Roman-style farms) were built in the valleys of the small rivers that run off the Chilterns, near the northern edge of the North Downs where springs emerge, and in the Darenth Valley. In some cases they are on or near the site of earlier native occupation; in others a new site seems to have been chosen. They are not to be found near Londinium, probably because prosperous men who farmed within easy reach of the city preferred to live in town. This land was in fact probably regarded as territory belonging to Londinium itself.

In south Essex there seem to have been few villas with much evidence of Romanized luxury, and people were living in native-style huts at Corbets Tye and Chelmsford in the 3rd century. It may be that a different form of land tenure was imposed on this territory, perhaps as a punishment for the part taken by the Trinovantes in the revolt of Boudicca. There seems to have been a prosperous villa in Wanstead Park, however, barely 6 miles from Londinium, where a mosaic pavement was found in 1715; and a substantial building at Abridge had the luxury of

Fig. 38 Mosaic floor of dining-room, Lullingstone Roman villa, showing Europa carried off by bull, mid-fourth century A.D.

under-floor heating.

Verulamium does not seem to have had quite the same influence as Londinium over the surrounding countryside, and villas developed in its neighbourhood—one, at Park Street, little more than 2 miles from the town. These, however, were already the sites of Belgic farms, probably owned by leading Catuvellaunian families. The pre-Roman owner of Park Street, for example, had a chain and manacle, and presumably kept slaves, although his dwelling was humble enough. Family tradition may have been stronger than the attraction of town life to these native aristocrats.

A number of villas had fine floors of mosaic, in which variously coloured small cubes of stone were arranged to make patterns and pictures (*fig. 38*). These occur in some Chiltern villas in the 2nd century, and were fairly common in the 4th century, which seems to have been a period of prosperity for the farmers. A more important refinement, for any farmer who regarded himself as a civilized Roman, was a bath-house, with a system of hot, warm and cold rooms, heated by hot air from a furnace passed under the floors. The same method of heating was also used for the main living-rooms. An interesting example is the villa at Gadebridge, on the outskirts of Hemel Hempstead. This was a wooden farmhouse that was rebuilt in stone in the late 2nd century as a corridor villa with projecting wings. Additions were made and a courtyard was enclosed. There had been a separate stone bath-house from the beginning and this was enlarged. Early in the 4th century, a great swimming bath, 21 metres by 12 metres, was constructed beside it. Extra rooms and heating arrangements were also added to the villa itself, which now seems to have been no longer a mere farmhouse, but possibly some kind of holiday hotel or spa. It was deliberately demolished after 353, according to coin evidence, and it is possible that the wealthy owner had been a supporter of the usurping Emperor Magnentius, who fell in that year.

The villa at Lullingstone, in the Darenth Valley, had in its final phase, after about 350, a Christian house-chapel, decorated with paintings of the Chi-Rho monogram of Christ and praying figures. At an earlier date the owners, then pagan, had built a round temple and a great tomb like a square Romano-Celtic temple. The family owning the villa at Keston, on the edge of the North Downs, had an even more impressive circular tomb of classical type, nearly 30 ft in diameter, with buttressed walls of flint. More in the native tradition are the conical barrows called the Six Hills near Stevenage, Herts, no doubt the burial places of descendants of the local Belgic aristocracy. Perhaps the mound in Morden Park, near Stane Street, is a Roman barrow of this kind.

OTHER RURAL SETTLEMENTS

Not all country settlements were Romanized farms. Riverside occupation of a humble character continued in places like Brentford, where remains of rectangular huts with wattle floors have been found on the foreshore, associated with pottery of the 2nd century A.D. At Tilbury, round wattle huts with plank flooring were occupied in early Roman times in a similar position, below present high-tide level. Small native settlements of this kind—presumably villages or hamlets—were no doubt to be seen in many places, not all by the river, but only in the favoured conditions of the foreshore have their remains survived in easily recognizable form. Unfortunately we know very little of the way such people lived, but fishing may have been as important as peasant farming for the riverside settlements. In many cases occupation seems to have continued on or near pre-Roman sites, and apart from the acquisition of Romanized goods life may have been little changed.

Temples were to be found in the countryside as well as in towns, and a square temple of Romano-Celtic type but with projecting annexes has been excavated at Harlow, Essex.

LATE ROMAN DEFENCES

In the 3rd century the peace of south-eastern Britain was increasingly disturbed by raids from Saxon pirates, who lived in the low country between the Rhine and the Elbe. A fort was built at Reculver about A.D. 210-20 to guard the approaches to the Thames Estuary, and it is possible that the wall of Londinium was intended as a protection against the same danger. A further development of coastal defences became necessary later in the century, and more forts were built to defend the shores vulnerable to these attacks, called the Saxon Shore. One of these was placed at Bradwell in Essex to overlook the estuary of the Blackwater, which also offered a convenient entry for the pirate ships. This fort has walls 12 ft thick at the base, and must have enclosed an area larger than 4 acres, although much of it has since been destroyed by erosion. There is a projecting tower called a bastion at the north west corner.

Bastions were a type of defence that became popular in later Roman times. Their purpose was to cover the approaches to the wall with the field of fire from a *ballista*—a spring-gun or catapult. Bastions were added to the city wall of Londinium, but we do not yet know at what date. The hollow bastions of the western part of the city are mediaeval, but the solid bastions of the eastern part may be late Roman. They contain many fragments of Roman monuments from the cemeteries used as building material to provide a solid core. One of these bastions recently investigated north of Aldgate seems to have been in existence in the late 4th century, for a deposit containing material of that date had accumulated against it. They may have been built as part of the military reconstruction which followed the disastrous barbarian attack on Britain in 367, when there were simultaneous invasions of the province by Saxons, Picts and Scots. Although Londinium was then in a state of siege, it never fell, and in 368 the city became the base of Theodosius, the Roman general who succeeded in clearing out the invaders and restoring the defences of Britain.

8 The Dark Age of London

THE END OF ROMAN BRITAIN

The term 'Dark Age' is not much liked by modern historians, but is still very appropriate to describe the obscurity which veils the London region in the centuries following the withdrawal of Roman power. Archaeology is beginning to throw a little light on the earlier years of this period, but the faint glimmer is soon lost, and for almost two centuries the archaeological record fails to confirm or correct the scanty information from unreliable historical sources.

Barbarian pressure increased, not only on Britain, but on the whole western world, and the Romans were further weakened by the attempts of usurpers to seize the Empire. First Magnus Maximus in 383 and then Constantine III in 407 withdrew armies from Britain to fight on the Continent, and in 410 the Emperor Honorius replied to a British plea for help against the Saxons with a letter saying that the cities of Britain would have to defend themselves. It is this final refusal of responsibility by the Emperor that is considered to mark the end of Roman rule in Britain; the last remaining Roman armies had left three years earlier.

The cities of Britain, with their local defence forces, did in fact succeed in keeping the barbarians at bay for years, so that Roman civilization survived for quite a long time in a Britain that was as independent of Roman rule as it had been before the Conquest. This is well illustrated by the story of St Germanus, Bishop of Auxerre, who came to Britain in 429 to fight the heresy of Pelagius. The latter was a Briton who had taught that men were free to choose good or evil for themselves, in opposition to the teaching of St Augustine that men could live a good life and save their souls only by the grace of God. Pelagius himself had left Britain many years earlier, but his belief was firmly established there, and seems to have taken on political overtones. British leaders who rejoiced in their new independence, and were prepared to come to terms with the Saxon invaders rather than lose it, probably tended to be Pelagians; whereas those who hoped for the return of Imperial authority preferred the views of Augustine. Germanus defeated the heretics in theological argument at a great assembly, almost certainly held at Verulamium, where he visited the shrine of St Alban, a Roman soldier who had been martyred there in one of the persecutions of the Christians. There is a reference to 'a man of tribunician rank' and to richly dressed, wealthy leaders, indicating that Verulamium was still prosperous and governed in Roman style. Germanus, who had been a successful soldier in his earlier life, then led the Britons to a great victory over a force of Picts and Saxons in a mountainous part of Britain. The barbarian horde was ambushed and routed to the war-cry of 'Alleluia'.

Fig. 39 Hot-room of Roman bath-house, Billingsgate, showing furnace arch and hypocaust

Archaeology has given us a glimpse, at both Verulamium and Londinium, of this survival of a prosperous Romano-British civilization amid the perils of the first half of the 5th century. At Verulamium a luxurious house was built after A.D. 364-7, on the evidence of a coin of that date found beneath one of its mosaic floors. It survived long enough for four structural alterations to be made. One of these included the installation of a corn-drying oven—an indication that some activities, that in more normal times would have been carried out in the countryside, were now being transferred to the greater safety of the town. A later development, probably for the same reason, was the demolition of the house and its replacement by a large building with buttresses, probably a barn or granary. All this suggests that corn was now brought within the city walls as quickly as possible. Finally, after the demolition of the barn itself, a wooden water-pipe was laid through its foundations. The wooden pipe had decayed, but the iron junctions of its sections remained at 6 ft intervals, marking its line. It can hardly have been laid much earlier than the mid-5th century, and provides evidence that the inhabitants of Verulamium were enjoying the amenity of piped water even at that date.

In Londinium, a comfortable house, with under-floor heating and its own private bath-suite, was occupied at the end of the 4th century on the north bank of the Thames to the east of the bridge, in what is now Billingsgate (*fig. 39*). More than 200 small bronze coins, including at least one of A.D. 395-402, were found scattered on the floor of the furnace room of the east wing. These coins included the last issues to reach Britain in bulk, which could not have been lost or deposited in a hoard much before A.D. 400. They could, of course, have been scattered where they were found at a much later date, but this must have been while the building was still intact. Another interesting piece of evidence actually lay beneath the uncleared ash of the furnace itself, from which hot air had passed beneath the floors of the living-rooms. This was a fragment of an amphora from Syria or Palestine, which had evidently been deposited while the under-floor heating was still in use, although probably not long before it was finally abandoned. It has been dated not earlier than A.D. 450 by Dr. J.W. Hayes, who based his judgment on the datable associations of this type of amphora in the Mediterranean.

If this date is correct, a riverside house in Londinium was still occupied at least into the third quarter of the 5th century. Moreover the occupants were not mere squatters camping on the premises, but people who were still trying to live in the Roman style with under-floor heating. Flue channels had been blocked, however, so that the heating was now apparently restricted to a single room. This may either indicate a shrunken household or lack of sufficient fuel to heat satisfactorily a suite of rooms. Perhaps for the same reason, the bath-house in its final phase (probably, but not certainly, coinciding with the final occupation of the house) was not used for its original purpose, and rubbish accumulated on the floor of its 'cold room'. Whatever their difficulties may have been, however, the final occupants of the house still had overseas connections and could afford to import wine, or some other luxury contained in the amphora, from the eastern Mediterranean when nearer sources of supply were cut off by barbarian invasions. Did they pay for it with what remained of the accumulated wealth of the past, or could Britain still produce exports for the London merchants? Slaves at least were readily available in times of trouble, and London was as convenient for this as for more honourable trades.

THE SUB-ROMAN COUNTRYSIDE

There are indications of continuing activity, both industrial and agricultural, in the countryside at the end of the 4th century or later. A coin of 388-402 was recently found in a corn-drying oven at Billericay, and coins of the same date were found in deposits contemporary with a structure that appeared to be a tile-kiln at Bow. A piece of glass associated with these finds is believed to be of the 5th century rather than the 4th. At Latimer in Buckinghamshire, a Roman villa building was abandoned towards the end of the 4th century, but a succession of timber and rubble buildings continued for many years on the site, taking its occupation well into the 5th century. The occupants kept pigs and cattle, although they also hunted deer for food. Their pottery was of Romano-British type, with shell-gritted ware becoming increasingly common. This ware was also found in the late levels at Billingsgate and Bow. The great difficulty about the study of this period, of course, is that when the coin evidence fails us, as it does about the end of the 4th century, we have no precise means of archaeological dating. There is Continental evidence of the dates of some small metal objects, such as buckles and brooches, and for the hand-made pottery of the Anglo-Saxon invaders, patiently studied for many years by Dr J.N.L. Myres, but we are not yet able to date closely the

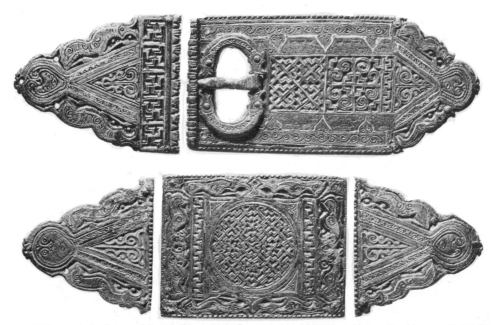

Fig. 40 Bronze belt-plates and buckle from Anglo-Saxon grave at Mucking, Essex, (Lengths overall, 16cm)

pottery in a late Roman tradition that occurs in 5th century levels. Much of it seems indistinguishable from late 4th century pottery, so that we cannot be certain that it is not a survival from that period.

EARLY ANGLO-SAXON SETTLERS

Until more progress is made with this study, we are obliged to judge the fate of the sub-Roman population mainly from the distribution of the Anglo-Saxon settlers at various dates. In the London region this is both curious and significant. At Mucking in Essex, on the Thames Estuary, and at Mitcham and Ham in Surrey, Anglo-Saxon pottery that can hardly be later than the early years of the 5th century has been found. Bronze buckles and other belt fittings of equally early date also occur in Anglo-Saxon graves at Mucking, Mitcham, Croydon and Orpington. These are of late Roman military type, ornamented in the barbaric style that appealed to Germanic taste (*fig. 40*). Military belt fittings of various forms, decorated in similar style, are also known from late Roman sites as early as the late 4th century, and have been convincingly explained as equipment for the German soldiers who were an important part of the defence forces of the late Roman Empire. From the time of Diocletian, it had been imperial policy to defend the frontiers against barbarian invasions by recruiting the barbarians themselves as soldiers, and giving them grants of land in return for their service. Military buckles in these late barbaric styles have been found in the Saxon-Shore fort of Bradwell, in Verulamium, Londinium, and in the Roman cemetery area just outside the walls of Londinium at Smithfield. There is little doubt that they belonged to soldiers recruited from one or other of the German tribes, such as the Franks, Alemanni, Friesians, or even the Saxons themselves, for the defence of these places in the last years of Roman rule. It has been suggested that some kinds of late Roman wheel-made pottery, decorated with ornamental bosses in Anglo-Saxon style, may have been intended to appeal to the taste of these barbarian soldiers and their families. Pottery of this kind has certainly been found in London and Essex, but even if it was influenced by Anglo-Saxon pottery of the period, and not merely by late Roman metal vessels, like the Anglo-Saxon pottery itself, it was not necessarily used only by people of German origin. The buckles, however, do suggest that such people were about, and that they were soldiers in the defence force, as seems to have been the case elsewhere.

Under the late Empire, a whole community or sub-tribe with its chief was often settled in a strategic area, where it held its land by treaty. It appears from later traditions that the same policy was pursued, with results that were eventually disastrous, by the Romanized Britons after they were told in 410 to organize their own defences. Power soon fell into the hands of military leaders, and one of these, named Vortigern, became supreme ruler of a large part of Britain, including the south-east. He was at first successful in protecting his territory by settling barbarian allies in the exposed eastern districts of the country.

In view of this policy of Vortigern and his predecessors, the early Anglo-Saxon communities at Mucking, overlooking the Thames Estuary, and on the southern land approaches to Londinium, must surely have been allies who had been permitted to settle, rather than invaders. The situation in the first half of the 5th century, therefore, seems to be that Romano-British life was continuing in Londinium and Verulamium, and in some country districts north of the Thames, probably including Bow, but that Anglo-Saxon settlements were already in full swing on the Thames Estuary and a few miles south of Londinium.

There is a striking contrast between the way of life of the Roman Britons of Billingsgate, with their centrally heated stone house, and that of the rough soldier-farmers of Mucking, 24 miles away. These mostly lived in squalid oblong huts, about 10 by 8ft, with floors sunk about 15 inches into the gravel, and two vertical posts to support a central ridgepole for the roof.

THE PROBLEM OF LONDON'S DARK AGE

Even with the early permitted Anglo-Saxon settlements a rigid system of *apartheid* seems to have been observed, and not a scrap of their characteristic hand-made pottery has been found in or near Londinium or Verulamium. As we have seen, it is likely that German mercenaries were employed in the defence forces of these towns, but these were probably recruited from a less barbarous people. The old connection between the Thames and the Rhine was probably still maintained, and it is quite likely that some of the defenders of Londinium itself were Franks, who had already adopted many Roman ways.

The Anglo-Saxon settlements south of the Thames increased in number in the 25 years or so before A.D. 450, for pottery of about this period has been identified at Northfleet—like Mucking, a site overlooking the Thames Estuary—at Orpington and Riseley in west Kent, as well as in a number of places in east Kent, including the Roman town of Canterbury itself. It has also been found on the north side of the river at Hanwell, west of London. Some is

very like pottery found in Frisia and in Jutland, and therefore gives a measure of archaeological support to the tradition, recorded by Bede, that the earliest English settlers in Kent were Jutes. These sites are on or near the old invasion route into Britain from the Straits of Dover, and may have been settled by invitation of Vortigern, not so much as a defence against other barbarians as against any attempt by the Roman armies still in Gaul to seize control of Britain again. Some of the traditional history of this time was written down about a century later by a monk called Gildas, and he tells us that an appeal for help was sent to the Roman general Aëtius about 446, evidently by the pro-Roman towns-people. No troops were actually sent, but there was a possibility that they might be; and St Germanus at least returned for a second visit, still full of zeal against the heretics, who probably included Vortigern, although he was now too old to lead the Britons in another 'Alleluia' victory.

According to the traditional history recorded by Gildas and Bede, Vortigern invited Hengist and Horsa to settle in the eastern part of Britain about this time or a few years earlier, to help in his defence, but they quarrelled with him, and Hengist fought two battles with the Britons. After the second of these at 'Crecganford'—probably Crayford—the defeated Britons fled 'in great fear' out of Kent to London. The date given by the Anglo-Saxon Chronicle for this event is 457. This may not be quite correct, but fits in with the known chronology. It now seems clear, however, that Hengist's settlement was the last of a series of such arrangements, and that similar Anglo-Saxon settlements for defensive purposes were in existence before his arrival. It also seems likely that there was a general revolt among all these mercenaries at this time.

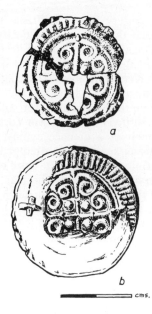

Fig. 41 Anglo-Saxon brooches, (a) from Billingsgate and (b) from Mitcham

Historians and archaeologists have argued for years about what happened to London next. Was it abandoned soon afterwards and left derelict for many years, or did its stout walls continue to give protection to Britons who tried to carry on the Roman city life of their fathers? Archaeology has not yet given a clear answer, for we have had a glimpse of this period only on one site, where stratified levels that seem to belong to the years after 450 survive only in a few places, and cannot easily be interpreted.

The Billingsgate house certainly *was* abandoned, probably soon after the piece of amphora found its way into the furnace room, since the ashes were never again cleared. It soon began to fall into ruins, probably as a result of neglect. First the windows were broken and fell in fragments on the floor; then wind and rain swept in, and eventually the roof-tiles were dislodged and fell in a heap on the floor. The more

strongly built vaulted roof of the bath-house, built of shaped hollow tiles mortared together, also collapsed, not necessarily at the same time. A rapid break-up of this roof through natural causes seems unlikely, but deliberate demolition at such a time is even more improbable. It had certainly fallen by the early years of the 6th century, if not much earlier, on the evidence of a much corroded circular brooch of pewter and bronze that was dropped into the roof debris after the collapse. It is almost identical with a brooch from a pagan Saxon woman's grave at Mitcham (*fig. 41*) where it was associated with a glass cone-beaker. Unfortunately neither is closely datable, and dates suggested by experts range from before 450 to well after 500. Most favour a date of about 450, and if this is correct, it is likely that the bath-house was a roofless shell by 475 at the latest. It is dangerous to generalize from the fate of one building, but the fact that an Anglo-Saxon woman could enter it, evidently on a scavenging expedition, strongly suggests that London was at that time derelict and undefended. Nevertheless, there is as yet no evidence at all of any Anglo-Saxon occupation of the city during this period, and the intrusion may have been merely a brief visit.

The Anglo-Saxons seem, in fact, to be missing from the greater part of our region north of the Thames in the late 5th and 6th centuries. South of the river, their pottery of this period is found at Northfleet, Keston, Orpington, Mitcham, Croydon, Ham and Walton Bridge, and just north of it at Shepperton, Hanwell and Mucking. Otherwise there seems to be hardly a trace of it in the northern part of our region, except on its outer edge in the Chilterns, at a time when Anglo-Saxon settlement was thick in East Anglia, and had extended along the Icknield Way into the Upper

Fig. 42 Early Anglo-Saxon church of St. Peter's-on-the-Wall, Bradwell-on-Sea, Essex, view from S.E. The nave is the only surviving portion, but the curved outline of the chancel apse can be seen on the ground

Thames Valley. The settlers seem to have avoided not only Londinium and Verulamium, but also the territory surrounding them for many miles. This has led to the suggestion that the sub-Roman population of this area still survived, and was capable of defending its land.

British resistance was by no means over, and Gildas tells us that a leader named Ambrosius Aurelianus defeated the Anglo-Saxons at a place called Badon Hill, checking their expansion for many years. This victory took place about 500, and although its greatest effect was on the west of Britain, it may also have relieved the pressure on London. The invaders certainly seem to have failed to establish new settlements in the London region north of the Thames in the 6th century. It has been suggested that Grim's Dykes, a series of stretches of bank and ditch in the Harrow district of north Middlesex, and a few miles south of the Icknield Way near Berkhampstead, might be defences and boundaries of this period. This may be correct, since excavation at a similar dyke on Brockley Hill in 1973 showed that it could not be earlier than the late Roman period. Unfortunately, in the absence of indentifiable pottery used by 6th century Londoners, archaeologists are not yet able to recognize their presence even in the city itself.

At Billingsgate, there is evidence of two constructive acts after the collapse of the roof of the Roman house. The first was the demolition and *deliberate removal* of the walls of its east wing. Only a small scatter of the ragstone remained nearby, as if it had fallen by accident from the cart that was removing it. This is an unlikely action for early Anglo-Saxon settlers, who had no tradition of building in stone. The second was the laying of a gravel surface, after a number of layers of silty earth had been deposited where the building had stood. Unfortunately it was not clear whether these had accumulated naturally over a long period of time as hill-wash, or whether they had been deliberately dumped to raise the level of the gravel surface just before it was laid. None of the pottery, either from the gravel or the underlying earth, is recognizably Anglo-Saxon. A very few sherds seem to be from hand-made pottery, but ware of this kind was found also in the sub-Roman levels at Latimer. The rest came from wheel-made pots, that are mostly indistinguishable, in our present state of knowledge, from pottery that was in use in the final phase of occupation of the Roman building. Other fragments may be of wares imported from the Continent in post-Roman times, but these await further study. It remains uncertain whether the removal of the walls and the laying of the gravel can be attributed to the 6th century, as the activities of the supposed sub-Roman population, or, following a period of abandonment, to the 7th century or later, when we know from historical sources that there was some revival of civilized life in London.

THE REVIVAL OF LONDON

The Londoners of the 7th century are, in fact, almost as elusive as those of the 6th, although events in early Church history, recorded by Bede, show that the city was certainly occupied. It was now dominated first by the Anglo-Saxon kings of Kent, and then by those of Essex. In 604 Augustine appointed Mellitus as Bishop of London, and the church of St Paul was built by Ethelbert, King of Kent. Mellitus was driven out in 616, however, when Kent and Essex returned to paganism. The East Saxons were then re-converted by Cedd,

Fig. 43 Early-Anglo-Saxon arch at church of All Hallows-by-the-Tower

Fig. 44 Anglo-Saxon gold coin minted in London, from the Crondall Hoard (enlarged, actual diameter 12mm.)

who became Bishop of London in 653. The little church that he built still stands over the west wall of the Roman fort at Bradwell on the Essex coast (*fig. 42*). After Cedd's death from plague about 664-5, the Bishopric of London and Essex was purchased by Wini. He was succeeded about 675 by Erkenwald, a great Bishop later remembered as 'The Light of London'. Erkenwald built abbeys at Barking and Chertsey, and may have been responsible for the one surviving piece of Anglo-Saxon architecture in London. In All Hallows-by-the-Tower, once the property of Barking Abbey, an arch formed of large tiles was revealed when the church was wrecked by bombing in 1940-1 (*fig. 43*). It is very much like arches in the church of Brixworth, Northants, built about 670 or a little later, and is likely to be of about the same date. There is also the corner of a wall formed with similar tiles. Both features are evidently parts of the London church of Barking Abbey, probably built in the late 7th or early 8th century.

Another indication of London's revival is the existence of gold coins actually minted in London in the mid-7th century, with the name LONDUNIU or LONDIOIIO upon them (*fig. 44*). It is clear that the return of the Church of Rome brought back other elements of Roman civilization, such as the art of building in stone and brick, a more sophisticated economy in which money was used as a means of exchange, and some degree of literacy. Written records were to become increasingly important as London became once more, in the words of Bede, 'a trading centre for many nations, coming to it by land and sea'. Archaeology continues to tell us a great deal about the new civilization that developed as London emerged from its Dark Age, but it is no longer our principal source of information.

Sites to Visit

The London region, being largely built-up or otherwise exploited by men in recent times, is not rich in archaeological field-monuments. Nevertheless, this is a selective list, in which only sites that are both easily accessible and readily recognizable have been included. In general, those that are on private property, to which access is given only as a special favour, have been omitted. An attempt has been made to represent as many periods and types of monument as possible within the chronological limits of this book, even at the cost of a little cheating in one or two instances, by passing just over the natural boundaries of the region (the ridges of the North Downs and Chilterns). Some of the things included are frankly unspectacular; others are of doubtful origin; but even those that hardly merit a special visit are sufficiently interesting to be sought out at a convenient time, perhaps in conjunction with some other business or pleasure. In compensation for these humbler sites, the list also contains a few of the most impressive monuments in Britain, worth a considerable effort to visit.

CITY OF LONDON

ALL HALLOWS-BY-THE-TOWER

ALL HALLOWS BARKING—also called
ALL HALLOWS-THE-GREAT

(*Fig. 45, 5*)
Date: Roman house—late 2nd century A.D. or later; Anglo-Saxon church architecture—late 7th-8th century A.D.
Map Ref: TQ334807
Position: 150 yards S.W. of Tower Hill District Railway Station, immediately W. of Tower of London, at E. end of Great Tower Street. (Can be conveniently combined with visit to eastern part of City Wall) *Access to crypt on application to the verger.*

Beneath the tower, near the bottom of the stairway to the crypt, is a Roman floor of red tesserae in its original position. It is divided by a gully that marks the position of a wooden wall, since decayed. A moulding in pink plaster with a light red surface remains at the junction of wall and floor. The red tesserae in the floor of the crypt further E. have been relaid below the level at which the floor was found. A section of a Roman wall of ragstone and flint, apparently contemporary with the floor, and probably of the same building, can be seen in the N. wall of the crypt.

The arch of the early Saxon church can be seen near the W. end of the S. wall of the nave, near the tower. It is built of flat tile-like bricks of Roman proportions, set on edge, not radially like a Roman arch, but sloping outwards.

Also of great interest, but beyond the scope of this book, are the fragments of

75

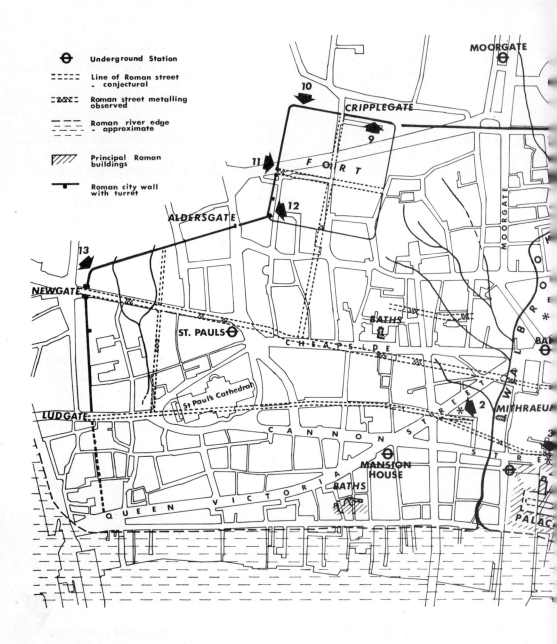

Fig. 45 Map of Roman London superimposed on street-plan of the modern City

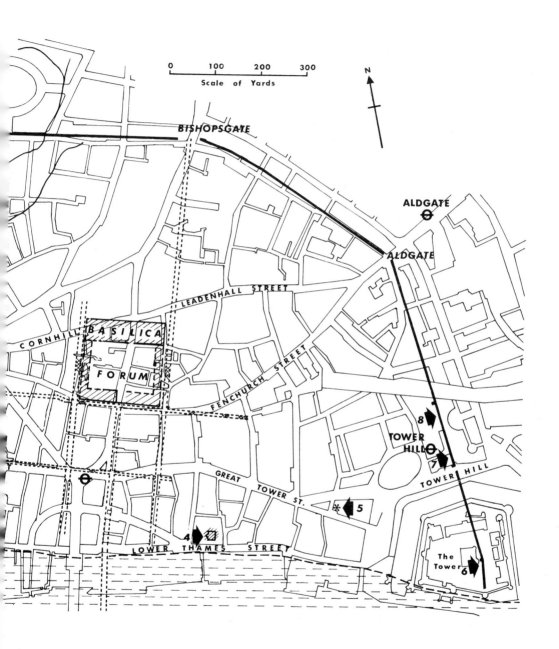

N

0   100   200   300
Scale of Yards

BISHOPSGATE

ALDGATE

ALDGATE

LEADENHALL STREET

CORNHILL

BASILICA

FORUM

FENCHURCH STREET

8

TOWER HILL

7

TOWER HILL

GREAT TOWER ST.

5

4

LOWER THAMES STREET

The Tower

6

three 11th century crosses exhibited in the crypt, with Roman finds from the site and elsewhere.

R. Merrifield, *The Roman City of London* (1965), 296f; *Antiquaries Journal* XXIII (1943), 15 ff.

BANK OF ENGLAND, THREADNEEDLE STREET

(Fig. 45,1)

MOSAIC FLOOR

Date: Roman, probably late 2nd or early 3rd century.
Map ref.: TQ327812
Position: Adjacent to the Bank Underground Station.
Access by permission, obtained by written application only.
A fine patterned mosaic floor, found on this site in 1933, can be seen from the Entrance Hall far below at the bottom of the main staircase. It is not in its original position. Another patterned mosaic, together with many well-preserved Roman objects found on this site, mostly in the bed of the Walbrook, is preserved in the Bank's private museum.
Journal of Roman Studies XXIV (1934), 211; XXV (1935), 216.

BILLINGSGATE (LOWER THAMES STREET)

(Fig. 45,4, Fig. 39)

ROMAN HOUSE WITH BATHS

Date: *c.* A.D. 200-450 (?)
Map ref.: TQ 332806
Position: N. side of Lower Thames Street, E. side of St Mary-at-Hill.
No access at present, but will be available for inspection after the development of the site.

The lower part of the bath-house and a portion of the E. wing of this late Roman house have been preserved. The furnace arch of the hot room, the brick supports of the floor and the box flue tiles in the wall can be seen, all forming part of a typical hypocaust heating system. In the warm room to the W., part of the Roman concrete floor remains, and there is a brick seat in the thickness of the wall. The unheated cold-room to the S. originally had a floor of red tesserae, part of which can be seen. Overlying a later floor a portion of the collapsed roof has been replaced as it was found, demonstrating the end of Roman London. The E. wing is separated from the bath-house by a corridor with floor of red tesserae. Flue channels from a separate furnace can be seen in the E. wing. These provided under-floor heating for the living rooms above. P.R.V. Marsden, *Londinium* (1971), 18 f, 38, 48.

ST BRIDES, FLEET STREET

ROMAN FLOOR

Map ref.: TQ 315811
Position: Off E. end of Fleet Street, S. side, W. of New Bridge St., near Blackfriars District Railway Station. *Access to crypt on application to the verger.*
The remains of an early church, probably mostly of the 11th century, have been preserved below the nave. The eastern apse overlay a pit containing a Late Saxon pottery handle. This had cut through the site of a Roman building with a floor of red tesserae, a small portion of which has been preserved E. of the apse. It is just visible reflected in the mirrors above the E. end of the early church. Tesserae and painted wall

plaster from the building are exhibited in a case.

The building was outside the walls of Londinium, in or adjacent to a Roman cemetery. It is possible, therefore, that it was a mausoleum or shrine, but there is no evidence that it was Christian.

The S.E. corner of a Roman ditched enclosure of early date was found under the N.W. part of the church.

W.F. Grimes, *The Excavation of Roman and Mediaeval London* (1968), 182 ff.

'LONDON STONE', CANNON STREET

(Fig. 45,3)
Date: Unknown: of pre-Mediaeval origin.
Map ref.: TQ 327809
Position: Now in S. wall of Bank of China, 111 Cannon Street; formerly in similar position in S. wall of St Swithin's Church, which occupied this site on the N. side of Cannon Street until its bombed ruins were demolished in 1960. Until 1742, however, it stood opposite on the S. side of Cannon Street, in a position now under the middle of the widened street. The surviving portion is an artificially rounded apex of Clipsham Limestone, little used in Roman times, and probably of post-Roman date. The Stone was already a landmark in the 12th century, however, and the veneration of it in the Middle Ages may have stemmed from an earlier tradition. Wren observed in excavations after the Fire of 1666 that it seemed to form part of a much larger structure. Its recorded position is in fact in the centre of a site likely to have been occupied by the outer gate of a Roman palace, probably the Governor's residence.
R. Merrifield, *Roman London* (1969), 95 ff.

'TEMPLE OF MITHRAS', RECONSTRUCTED

(Fig. 45,2)
Date: Modern, built mainly of Roman material.
Map ref.: TQ 325811
Position: On a terrace outside Temple Court, 11 Queen Victoria Street. Near the Bank and Cannon Street Underground Stations.

This is a full-sized ground-plan of the Roman building excavated in 1954 on the site of Bucklersbury House, Walbrook, about 60 yards to the S.E. It shows in plan the nave, side aisles, sleeper walls with settings for column-bases, and sanctuary within a buttressed apse, as they were found in the original structure, from the material of which it has been built. It is not an accurate reconstruction in three dimensions, however, as differences of level have mostly been disregarded, so that the rebuilt structure is much flatter than the original. It should also be noted that it is on a different alignment (N.—S. instead of E.—W.). In several instances the use of material is misleading; floors of earth and wood are represented by crazy paving, and a wooden water tank by a structure built of ragstone from the walls. The most interesting feature is the original worn door-step, with iron collars for the door pivots still in their sockets.
W.F. Grimes, *The excavation of Roman and Mediaeval London* (1968), 92 ff, 230 ff.

ROMAN CITY WALL

Date: *c.* A.D. 200
Only the sites accessible to the public at

certain times, at all times, or by arrangement, are given below. The Roman city wall has been preserved also in the basements of private property on other sites, not normally accessible to the public. These have been omitted, as have portions of the city wall where no Roman work is visible.

EASTERN PORTION

Map ref.: TQ 336805-336808
Position: Within a few minutes walk of Tower Hill District Railway Station; in Tower of London and also east of Cooper's Row.
R. Merrifield. *The Roman City of London* (1965), 155 ff, 299 ff.

(1) TOWER OF LONDON

(Fig. 45,6) A stretch of the base of the Roman city wall, about 10½ ft long, is preserved to the east of the White Tower, behind the ruins of the Wardrobe Tower. The lower part of the latter was originally a bastion of the wall, of uncertain date. A triple course of tiles forms an off-set on the inner face of the city wall; above this is a facing of squared blocks of ragstone, and then a triple course of bonding tiles that runs through the thickness of the wall.

(2) TOWER HILL

N. side. (Fig. 45,7) A fine piece of city wall on the E. side of a sunken garden, the surface of which is at Roman ground level. The upper part is mediaeval, but the core of the Roman wall survives to about 1 foot above modern pavement level. At the N. end is a well-preserved inner face of Roman wall, with triple facing-course of tiles at the base, and three tile bonding courses above, with facing courses of ragstone blocks between them. S. of this the face has gone, and the rubble core is exposed. At the S. end, half of the base of an internal Roman tower can be seen in the grass.

In the adjacent Wakefield Gardens is a cast of the inscription from the tomb of Classicianus, found in a bastion nearby (see p. 53). The composite statue of a Roman Emperor is a 19th century copy, unconnected with Roman London.

(3) COOPER'S COURTYARD BEHIND MIDLAND HOUSE (NOS. 8-10 COOPER'S ROW)

(Fig. 45,8) A fine piece of Roman and mediaeval city wall, surviving to its mediaeval parapet, with window and loop-holes for archers (of about A.D. 1200) in the upper part. The Roman wall below rises from the original ground surface, at the level of the basement car park, to 2½ ft above the courtyard floor—a height of about 13 ft. The inner Roman facing of ragstone blocks survives at two levels. On the outside the sandstone plinth can be seen, corresponding in level to the triple facing-course of tiles on the inside. The arch through the wall is recent.

NORTHERN PORTION

Map ref.: TQ 324816-325816
Position: West of Moorgate Underground station, north of the double carriage-way of London Wall. (A piece of purely Roman city wall is preserved in the underground car park under the double carriage-way west of Coleman Street, but can be visited only by users of the car park.) W.F. Grimes, *The Excavation of Roman and Mediaeval London* (1968), 15 ff, 47 ff.

(1) LONDON WALL, ST ALPHAGE CHURCHYARD

(Fig. 45,9) The city wall here shows much of

the history of London's fortifications to the last major rebuilding of 1476-7, when the battlements of diaper brick-work were constructed. Below these, various mediaeval rebuildings can be seen on the outside of the wall. One of ashlar, containing courses of knapped flint and tiles, seems to be of the mid-14th century. At the base the wall is Roman, though of different character from the normal Roman wall. It consists, in fact, of two walls, as can be seen in section at the E. end of this stretch. The outer, to the N., is what remains of the fort wall of the early 2nd century; the inner is the thickening added when the N. wall of the fort was incorporated in the city wall. The outer side was reduced and re-faced with masonry at some unknown but early period.

(2) ST GILES' CRIPPLEGATE

(Fig. 45,10) South of the churchyard of St Giles and a modern 'moat' is a stretch of city wall recently cleared of the modern ruins of the last war that adjoined it. The wall here was badly damaged by the enlargement of later cellars, and much of the inner side has been cut away. The lower portion is Roman, but considerable restoration has been necessary. The remains of the bastion on the N. side overlay 13th century pottery, and are therefore mediaeval, as must also be the great corner bastion and the bastions to the S. of it, which are of similar build. One of these, Bastion 14, still stands just to the N. of the double carriage-way of London Wall. The corner bastion marks the place where the wall changes direction through 90°, because it incorporates here the N.W. corner of the rectangular Roman fort of earlier date.

WEST SIDE OF ROMAN FORT

Date: Early 2nd century, with city wall addition of c.A.D. 200.

Map ref.: TQ 322815

Position: Underlying double carriage-way of London Wall just E. of Aldersgate Street, and also on W. side of Noble Street S. of London Wall. A few minutes' walk to the north of St Paul's Underground Station.

W.F. Grimes, *The Excavation of Roman and Mediaeval London* (1968), 15 ff.

(1) LONDON WALL, END OF UNDERGROUND CAR PARK

(Fig. 45,11) A stairway on the N. side of London Wall, opposite Noble Street, gives access to the W. gate of the Roman fort, open from 12.30 to 2 p.m., Monday to Friday, except Bank Holidays; for parties at other times by arrangement with the Director of Guildhall Museum.

The northern half of the lower portion of the west gate of the early 2nd century Roman fort (see p. 56f) is preserved, with central piers and guard-room of rectangular N. tower, which has an external sandstone plinth. Adjoining the N. side of the tower is a short stretch of a double ragstone wall. The outer, on the W. side, is the original wall of the fort; the inner is the thickening that was built to reinforce it when it was incorporated in the city wall about A.D. 200. The gateway was a double one, with two outer doors, and the slots for the posts of the northern one can be seen. At an unknown but early period, perhaps in later Roman times, the gateway was blocked by a rough wall, which has been left in position on the S. side.

(2) NOBLE STREET, W. SIDE

(Fig. 45,12) Portions of the double Roman wall, consisting of outer fort wall of the early 2nd century and inner thickening added about A.D. 200, when it became part of the city wall, can be seen at basement level, divided into short sections by the cellar walls of the 19th century buildings destroyed in the last war. Only the inner thickening is visible in many places, but both walls can be seen adjoining a small rectangular internal turret 50 yards S. of London Wall. Farther S., opposite Oat Lane, both can be seen again. The inner thickening comes to an end here, and the outer (fort) wall curves to the S.E. at the rounded S.W. corner of the fort, within which is a corner turret. Adjoining the corner on the W. is a portion of the base of the city wall, which here swings away to the S.W., making an obtuse angle with the W. wall of the fort. The fort ditch, cut in the natural brick-earth, can be seen below the piece of city wall, which blocks it. In the wall is a brick culvert, evidently built to replace the blocked ditch as a drain. A short piece of wall adjoining the outside of the fort wall a few yards to the N. is a remnant of a hollow bastion, similar to the mediaeval bastions N. of London Wall.

WESTERN CORNER

Map ref.: TQ 319814
Position: 300 yards W. of St Paul's Underground Station, just N. of Newgate Street opposite the Central Criminal Court. Access only by arrangement. *Apply in advance to the Postmaster, the G.P.O., St Martin's-le-Grand. Archaeologia* LXIII (1912), 286 ff.

GENERAL POST OFFICE YARD E. OF GILTSPUR STREET

(Fig. 45,13) (*Access only by permission— see above*). A curved portion of the N.W. corner of the city wall with a hollow bastion adjoining its western end is preserved in a compartment under the yard, with its base 12 ft below the modern surface. It has the usual construction of the Roman wall outside the fort area, with a facing of squared ragstone blocks in regular courses, and double bonding-courses of tiles running through the wall, which is 7¾ ft thick above the plinth. It had apparently tilted outwards and cracked before the bastion was added. The latter is presumably mediaeval, like the other hollow bastions. It is of ragstone set in white mortar, with a carefully smoothed outer face, and contained no re-used stones.

BEDFORDSHIRE

DUNSTABLE DOWN—FIVE KNOLLS

BURIAL MOUNDS
Date: Late Neolithic—Early Bronze Age.
Map ref.: TL 007210
Position: On Dunstable Down, ¼ mile S. of junction of Icknield Way (B489) and road to Whipsnade (B4541).
This prehistoric cemetery consists of two bowl-barrows, three bell-barrows within one ditch, and two suspected pond-barrows. The more northerly bowl-barrow is the only one that has been properly excavated. It contained a crouched female skeleton with a polished flint blade of the Late Neolithic period. A secondary cremation burial in a collared urn was added in the Early Bronze Age. A reconstruction of the primary burial is exhibited in Luton Museum.

WAULUD'S BANK, LEAGRAVE

DEFENSIVE OR CEREMONIAL ENCLOSURE
Date: Late Neolithic.
Map ref.: TL 062246
Position: ¼ mile N. of Leagrave Railway Station, reached by footpath on E. side of the River Lea.
The bank and ditch form a semi-circular

enclosure of about 18 acres, with the River Lea, which rises within it, completing the circuit on the W. side.

An excavation in 1953 produced Late Neolithic grooved ware from the ditch floor, and the post-holes of a hut were found on the outer edge of the ditch. The site was evidently the tribal centre of Late Neolithic herdsmen who occupied this part of the Chilterns.

Current Archaeology (Jan., 1972) 173 ff.

BUCKINGHAMSHIRE

CHOLESBURY

HILL-FORT

Date: 2nd century B.C. refortified in the 1st century A.D.

Map ref.: SP 930073

Position: On N. side of the village, 2¾ miles S. of Tring (S. from A41).

This fort is oval in plan with two banks and ditches on the N. side and three on the S. (damaged near the village street). It has been excavated and the finds are in Aylesbury Museum.

GERRARDS CROSS (BULSTRODE PARK CAMP)

HILL FORT:

Date: *c*. 1st century B.C.

Map ref.: SU 995880

Position: In the W. angle of Gerrards Cross, made by the A40 and A332, ½ mile S.W. of Gerrards Cross Railway Station.

This fort is oval in shape, with a single ditch and inner bank, 12 ft high in places, and a slight outer bank, enclosing about 22 acres. It is not yet known which of the three gaps is the original entrance. This hill-fort does not seem to have been permanently occupied.

GRIM'S DITCH, CHILTERNS

LINEAR EARTHWORK

Date: Uncertain (?) Early Iron Age or

Dark Age.

Map refs.: SP830014-838030-846026, 900073, 917087-940095

Position: W. of Hampden House, Little Hampden: W. of road from Wendover to St Leonards: W. of road from Wigginton to Cholesbury.

This was formerly thought to belong to the Dark Age, but more recently has been believed to be a tribal boundary of the later pre-Roman Iron Age. (See comment on Middlesex Grim's Dyke, however, p. 72).

ESSEX

AMBRESBURY BANKS (EPPING FOREST)

HILL-FORT

Date: Early Iron Age, *c*. 2nd-1st century B.C.

Map ref.: TL 438003

Position: On N.E. edge of Epping Forest, adjacent to A11 (S.E. side) about 1¾ miles S.W. of centre of Epping. The N. side of the rampart can be seen from the road.

This earthwork encloses 11 to 12 acres, and consists of a single bank and ditch, with traces of a slight external bank in places. Excavation has shown that the ditch, now almost filled with leaf-mould, is V-shaped, 22 ft wide at the top, and 10 ft deep. The in-turned entrance on the S.E. side is now known to be mediaeval. The original entrance is a stone-lined gap at the centre of the W. side.

BRADWELL-ON-SEA

ROMAN SHORE FORT AND SAXON CHAPEL

Dates: Late 3rd century and *c*. A.D. 654.

Map ref.: TM031082

Position: On the edge of salt marshes S. of the mouth of the Blackwater. Reached by minor road and track—a Roman road— (no cars allowed on the final track) from

Bradwell-on-Sea.

H.M. Carter, *The Fort of Othona and the Chapel of St. Peter-on-the-Wall, Bradwell-on-Sea, Essex.* 1966, (Guide-book).

(1) ROMAN FORT OF SAXON SHORE

More than half has been eroded by the sea, leaving about 3 acres enclosed by the W. wall and parts of the N. and S. walls. The Chapel almost certainly stands on the site of the W. gate. There is little to be seen except part of the S. wall, 4-5 ft high and about 12 ft thick, and only a few feet of the masonry of the S. face are exposed. This can be seen near the cottage. There is an off-set course of tiles at the foot over the wider concrete foundation; then three courses of stone with a triple course of bonding-tiles above. There is an external ditch, here close to the wall. This fort, probably built under Carausius, is almost certainly the *Othona* of the Antonine Itinerary.

(2) SAXON CHAPEL
(Fig. 42)

In the little Chapel of St Peter-on-the-Wall, a surprising amount of the church built by St Cedd about 654 remains, after use for many years as a barn. The surviving portion is the nave, 50 by 22 ft internally. The church originally had also a western porch, eastern apse, and a porticus (side-chamber) on each side adjoining the apse and E. end of the nave. The position of the apse can be clearly seen in the grass; and part of the wall of the S. porticus is exposed. Portions of two arches, built with re-used flat Roman bricks, survive in the E. wall of the nave—the outer wall of the present chapel. There are the remains of external buttresses, and the junctions of the walls of porch, side-chambers and apse can also be seen on the outside of the wall.

LOUGHTON CAMP (EPPING FOREST)

HILL-FORT
Date: Early Iron Age, *c.*2nd-1st century B.C.
Map ref.: TQ 419975
Position: Hidden in Epping Forest. Leave A11 at Robin Hood Inn, and approach from track between Earl's Path and Clay Road. A good map and *compass* are essential, especially for the return journey. Making a circuit of Loughton Camp without a compass is as quick a way as any of getting lost in the forest.
The earthwork consists of a single bank and ditch, and encloses about 6½ acres. There are various gaps, but the position of the original entrance is unknown. The fortification is slight on the S.W. side, where there is a steep natural slope.

PRITTLEWELL, PARISH CHURCH OF ANNUNCIATION

ANGLO-SAXON ARCH
Date: (?) 7th or 8th century.
Map ref.: TQ877868
Position: Victoria Avenue, Southend-on-Sea (conveniently visited with Museum, Prittlewell Priory.)
Half of the arch of a blocked door, built of flat tile-like bricks of Roman type, can be seen both on the outside and inside of the N. Wall of the chancel. Excavation in 1954 showed that the internal height of the arch from the door-step was 6 ft 2 in., identical with that of St Martin, Canterbury. The S. wall of the early church was found in 1952, 22 ft S. of the N. wall. It was built of blocks of Kentish ragstone surfaced with plaster, with a rubble foundation of gravel, flint and ragstone. It is possible that this church was built in the time of Cedd.
E.N. Gowing, *The Story of Prittlewell Church* (1958) 8 ff.

HERTFORDSHIRE

REDBOURN, THE AUBREYS

LOWLAND (PLATEAU) FORT

Date: Early Iron Age, possibly of 1st century B.C.
Map ref.: TL095112
Position: N. and W. of junction of M1 and B487. Can be seen in passing from the northbound lane of the M1, or more conveniently from the minor road from Holtsmere End to Redbourn.
It consists of a double bank and ditch on all sides except the N.W., which may be unfinished. Here there is a single bank and ditch. The two entrances seem to have been to the W. and N.W., at the ends of the stretch of single bank and ditch. The fort encloses about 18 acres and commands the River Ver.

ST ALBANS, BEECH BOTTOM DYKE

BELGIC BOUNDARY DYKE

Date: 1st century B.C.—1st century A.D.
Map ref.: TL146087-162095
Position: Extends along N. edge of Townsend School playing-field, eastward under A6 and N.E. under trees to railway. Beyond the railway it continues N.E. to B651. It is best seen just E. of A6 at TL150088.
The Ditch today is 29 ft deep and 90 ft wide in places, but the original depth is not known. Its main bank is on the S. side, so it is evidently a northern boundary. A coin hoard of the early 2nd century was found in its fill, indicating that the Ditch had by that date passed out of use. It seems likely that it was a boundary associated with the pre-Roman Catuvellaunian capital at Prae Wood.
R. E. M. and T. V. Wheeler, *Verulamium, a Belgic and Two Roman Cities*, (1936), 16 ff.

STEVENAGE, SIX HILLS

ROMAN BARROWS

Map ref.: TL237237
Position: In a row beside the Great North Road (A1), which here overlies a minor Roman road, on the S.W. side of Stevenage.
These are large steep-sided round barrows, about 60 ft in diameter and 10 ft in height. They have not been scientifically excavated, but their size, shape and position beside a Roman road indicate that they are of Roman date.

VERULAMIUM (ST ALBANS), ROMAN TOWN

(The Verulamium Museum, which must not be missed, can be the starting point for the following visits.)

(1) THEATRE
(Fig. 35)
Date: Mid-2nd century A.D., rebuilt early 3rd century.
Map ref.: TL134074
Position: W. of A414, St Albans to Hemel Hempstead, immediately N.W. of St Michael's Church. Privately owned, small admission charge, open 10 a.m. to dusk.
The external bank on which the visitor walks is not part of the structure, but the dump of earth excavated from it. From it can be seen the external wall and the buttressed wall that supported the auditorium bank, represented by modern grassed banks. Three gangways, originally vaulted over to carry more seats, give access to an almost circular central area, which adjoined the stage. A single column of the line of three behind the stage has been reconstructed. The circular area was probably sometimes used as a small

amphitheatre. Theatres of this type are often associated with temples, however, as in this case, and it is possible that religious ceremonies were also held in the central area.

Archaeologia LXXXIV (1934), 213 ff.

(2) ROMAN SHOPS AND TOWN HOUSE

Date: Mid-1st and second half of 2nd century A.D.
Map ref.: TL135074
Position: S.E. of Theatre, within Theatre enclosure; conveniently viewed on the same occasion.

The lay-out of the wall-footings of pre-Boudiccan houses and shops adjacent to Watling Street, excavated 1957-60, have been marked in concrete. To the S., part of a large town house, built after A.D. 155, can be seen. A notable feature is an underground shrine, with an apse, presumably for a cult statue, and a niche for a lamp.

Ilid Anthony, *Verulamium* (1970) (Guidebook), 9 ff.

(3) BASILICA

Date of original building: A.D. 79 (from inscription in Museum).
Map ref.: TL136073
Position: The Basilica (Court of Justice and Town Hall) lies partly under St Michael's Church. The position of its N.E. corner, with one of the offices or shops on its N. side has been marked in the grass on the W. side of the Museum.

(4) HYPOCAUST AND MOSAIC FLOOR

Date: *c*.A.D. 150-190, partly rebuilt about A.D. 300.
Map ref.: TL136069
Position: In Park, 450 yards S. of Museum.
Open 10 a.m., Sunday 2 p.m., closed at 5.30 p.m., 1st March-31st October; November-February, weekends only, closing at 4 p.m. A large mosaic pavement with a hypocaust heating system beneath it is protected by a modern brick bungalow. It formed part of the bath wing of a large town house 200 ft long and 130 ft wide. The eastern part of the Roman town, most of it as yet unexcavated, underlies the Park.

R. E. M. and T. V. Wheeler, *Verulamium: a Belgic and two Roman Cities* (1936) 102 ff.

(5) CITY WALL

Date: About A.D. 200 or a little later.
Map ref.: TL137067
Position: 750 yards S. of Museum, N. of King Harry Lane.
The wall is built of flint, with triple courses of tiles running horizontally through the wall at vertical intervals of about 3 ft. It is about 7 ft thick at ground level, with foundations considerably thicker, and probably originally stood to a height of more than 20 ft. Outside the wall is the ditch, which becomes double on the S.W. side, where the ground is flat. There is a 15 ft level space between the wall and ditch. Two square internal towers built at the same time as the wall can be seen. There are also bastions projecting on the outside of the wall, and the relationship of these to the original wall is not clear. They appear to be bonded into it, but it is more likely that they are of later date, and were bonded into a wall-face that had already decayed.
Portions of the E. wall can also be seen near the lake.

R.E.M. and T.V. Wheeler, *loc. cit.*, 58 ff.

(6) THE LONDON GATE

Modern lay-out of plan of (?) 2nd century gate.
Map ref.: TL138067
Position: At the point E. of the city wall described above (5) where Watling Street

86

entered the Roman city, about 700 yards S. of Museum.

The plan of the S.W. or London Gate is marked in the grass with modern flint-work above its buried foundations. There are two carriage-ways and two passages for pedestrians, with projecting rounded towers on either side. This gateway was built before the city wall, and is believed to have been the monumental gate of the earlier earthwork defences that were replaced by the wall. It continued in use as the main S. gate.

R. E. M. and T. V. Wheeler, *loc. cit.*, 63 ff.

WHEATHAMPSTEAD, DEVIL'S DYKE AND THE SLAD

BELGIC OPPIDUM

Date: 1st century B.C.
Map refs.: TL183133, 188133
Position: ½ mile S.E. of Wheathampstead town centre.

It has been suggested that these two massive dykes formed part of a single earthwork, enclosing nearly 100 acres. The western dyke (Devil's Dyke) was excavated, and found to be 40 ft deep and at one point 130 ft wide. The material from the ditch had been piled to form a bank 9 ft high on the E. side, and another 6ft high on the W. side. (See fig. 27) The Slad has not been excavated, and doubts of its artificial nature have been expressed. The site is of strategic value, since it dominates a ford over the Lea. It has been suggested that this was the tribal headquarters of Cassivellaunus, attacked by Julius Caesar in 54 B.C.

R. E. M. and T. V. Wheeler, *loc. cit.*, 16 ff.

KENT
LONDON BOROUGH OF BROMLEY

KESTON

ROMAN MAUSOLEUM AND TOMBS

Date: Early 3rd century A.D. and later.
Map ref.: TQ415632
Position: On 146 bus route from Bromley South Station, on hillside adjoining the Foreign Bird Farm at Warbank, Keston; motorists take A233. (Arrangements to visit are made with the Manager, Keston Foreign Bird Farm Ltd., Brambletye, Westerham Road, Keston, Kent. Tel: Farnborough 52351.)

The most imposing monument is a circular buttressed mausoleum about 29 ft in diameter, built of flint and tile. Only the lower part survives, and it probably originally stood 20-30 ft high, as a drum-shaped structure surmounted by an earth mound. An adjacent rectangular tomb about 15 by 11 ft has a single buttress. The space between two of the buttresses of the circular mausoleum has been partly enclosed with a curved wall and used as the tomb for a cremation. Here, no doubt, was the family burial ground of the owner of the villa, partly excavated but again covered, on the lower slopes of the hill.

Just to the N.E. in Holwood Park is a fine Early Iron Age *hill-fort* with 2-3 lines of rampart and ditch, but this is unfortunately not accessible to the public. A second earthwork, possibly a cattle-pound, can be seen on the W. side of the road, however, on Keston Common (TQ418642)

Current Archaeology (May, 1969), 73 ff.

ORPINGTON

ROMAN BUILDING, PRESUMABLY A VILLA

Map ref.: TQ454659
Position: Just W. of Orpington Station, projecting from bank below the Borough Council Offices.

Flint walls, a threshold, and floors of coarse red tesserae, evidently of a substantial Roman building can still be seen where they were excavated. They are too fragmentary to merit a special visit from a distance, but are worth notice when in the neighbourhood.

Archaeologia Cantiana, LXXI 240, LXXII, 210.

LONDON BOROUGH OF GREENWICH

GREENWICH PARK

(1) ROMAN FLOOR

Map ref.: TQ392774
Position: The Roman building lies in the eastern part of the Park, about 100 yards from the E. wall, half-way between the Vanbrugh and Maze Hill gates.
Only a tiny piece of floor of coarse red tesserae can be seen, preserved in a small enclosure among trees. Very little is known of this building, but rather unusual finds have come from it, including a fragment of sculpture and several small pieces of different inscriptions. It is possible that it was a temple of some kind rather than an ordinary villa, but not enough has been recovered of the ground plan to indicate the nature of the building. About 300 coins found here ranged from Claudius to Honorius, but were mostly early 4th century.

Royal Commission on Historical Monuments, *An Inventory of the Historical Monuments in London,* vol. III.*Roman London* (1928), 151.

(2) BARROWS, SAXON (?)

Date: (?) Second half of 6th century.
Map ref.: TQ388771
Position: In western part of Park, W. of Observatory Building and N.W. of reservoir. A number of small barrows can still be seen. They are about 12-15 ft in diameter, with traces of ditches around them. The higher ones stand about 2 ft above present ground level. Originally there were more, since a number are known to have been destroyed in the last two centuries.

Finds recorded in 1784 show that this was the site of a rather late and impoverished Pagan Saxon cemetery. The bodies were buried in coffins, and traces of woollen cloth and a braid of hair were found. There were also glass beads of various colours, a large iron spearhead and the iron boss of a shield. In 1846, however, stone implements are said to have been found in the barrows, so it is possible that they are Early Bronze Age barrows re-used for Saxon burials.
Transactions of Greenwich and Lewisham Antiquarian Society (1929), 166 ff.

KENT
OUTSIDE LONDON

ADDINGTON

(Strictly speaking these are just outside the London Region, being S. of the ridge of the North Downs, as is Coldrum tomb-chamber.)

LONG BARROW AND 'CHESTNUTS' BURIAL CHAMBER

Date: Neolithic.
Map ref.: TQ653591 and 652592
Position: The Long Barrow bestraddles the minor road from Addington to Wrotham Heath (N. of A20) and is very near Addington Church. The 'Chestnuts' burial chamber lies 50 yards to the N.W. A cluster of stones on the N. side of the road probably comes from the collapsed burial chamber, or possibly from a false entrance. The line of smaller stones on the S. side of the road are the remains of the retaining wall on the S.E. side of the barrow, and a similar line parallel to it on either side of the road represents the corresponding wall on the N.W. side. The whole barrow was about 200 ft long and 40 ft wide, with a N.E.—S.W. orientation.

The 'Chestnuts' ruined burial chamber 50 yards to the N. is a more spectacular group of stones, but has been badly damaged. The rest of this barrow has disappeared, and its shape cannot be traced.

R. F. Jessup, *The Archaeology of Kent* (1930), 70 ff.

COLDRUM

CHAMBERED LONG BARROW

Date: Neolithic.
Map ref.: TQ654607
Position: 600 yards S. of Pilgrim's Way. Best reached by minor road and track E. from village of Trottiscliffe (E. from A227 N.E. of Wrotham).

The lines of sarsen stones mark the walls of the barrow which, for a long barrow, is unusually short (90 ft) for its breadth (50 ft). A rectangular stone burial chamber stands towards the E. end of the enclosure, which was once covered by a mound. The cap-stone of the chamber has gone. (One can be seen in position at Kits Coty, 5½ miles to the E.—not included here as it is E. of the Medway.) Excavations in 1910 and 1922 showed that at least 22 individuals had been buried at different times in this communal tomb. One skull, evidently of an important person, was placed in a special position on two blocks of stone.

R.F. Jessup, *loc. cit.*, 72 ff.

LULLINGSTONE

ROMAN VILLA

Date: Late 1st—early 5th century.
Map ref.: TQ529651
Position: On W. bank of Darenth. Continue on A225 just over 200 yards S. of Eynsford Station; turn right on minor road to N.W. (½ mile) across river to villa. The villa as excavated has been preserved under a protective structure, where finds from the site are also exhibited. Small admission charge. May-September, open daily 9.30 a.m.-5.30 p.m. Other months, open daily, but shorter hours and Sunday afternoons only.

This is one of the finest villas in Britain. There is a splendid mosaic of Europa and the bull, with two lines of Latin verse, in the Dining-Room; and another of Bellerophon killing the Chimaera, with symbolic pictures of the Seasons, in the Reception Room. These were laid about A.D. 330-50. At the S. end is a bath-suite; and the N. end was used for religious purposes. A 'Deep Room', at one time devoted to a cult of local Water Goddesses, was covered by a room that was converted into a Christian chapel about A.D. 370, on the evidence of its painted wall plaster with Christian symbols and praying figures. On the hill-side behind are the remains of a circular temple of the 2nd century and a temple-like mausoleum, beneath which a young man and woman were buried about A.D. 300.

G. W. Meates, *Lullingstone Roman Villa* (1955); also Guide-book (1962).

SWANSCOMBE—BARNFIELD PIT

SECTION THROUGH PLEISTOCENE LOAM, SAND AND GRAVEL OF THE 100 FT TERRACE OF THE THAMES

Date: Lower Palaeolithic.
Map ref.: TQ596744
Position: S. from Swanscombe Halt, turning W. at fork to disused chalk-pit, now a Nature Reserve. It is best seen near the S.W. corner of the pit, in the section facing W.

Although this is purely a geological section, many archaeologists will wish to visit the classic site that produced the only human remains of Lower Palaeolithic man as yet found in Britain, and a wealth of Palaeolithic implements, especially of the Middle Acheulian Industry.

In the section can be seen at the top grey hill wash; then gravel and loam, the 'Upper

Gravel', believed to be of the Gipping glacial period; then sand of the top of the 'Upper Middle Gravel', with gravel of the 'Lower Middle Gravel' below it. The skull of Swanscombe Man came from the 'Middle Gravel' farther to the E.

J. Wymer, *Lower Palaeolithic Archaeology in Britain* (1968), 334 ff.

MIDDLESEX
LONDON BOROUGH OF CAMDEN

PARLIAMENT HILL

ROUND BARROW (?)

Date: Unknown. Possibly Bronze Age.
Map ref.: TQ274865
Position: 300 yards N.E. of N. end of Hampstead Ponds.

This mound is 110-120 ft in diameter, and about 10 ft high. It was drawn by Stukeley in 1725, and there is little doubt that it is of some antiquity. Its appearance suggests that it is a Bronze Age barrow, but excavation in 1894 showed that the external ditch is comparatively modern. There is, however, a buried ditch inside its circuit, and this is probably part of the original structure. It was also shown that additions had been made to the top of the mound in the last few centuries. No human remains were found, but near the centre of the mound was an irregular pocket of charcoal, at a depth of 6 ft 6 in. from the upper surface, extending downwards for 18 in. and resting on the original ground surface. Pits containing charcoal, presumably from a funeral pyre, are sometimes found in Bronze Age barrows, but the nature of this earthwork will remain uncertain unless further evidence can be obtained.

C. E. Vulliamy, *The Archaeology of London and Middlesex* (1930), 274 ff.

LONDON BOROUGH OF HARROW
PINNER GREEN — GRIM'S DYKE OR DITCH (1)

LINEAR EARTHWORK

Date: uncertain (?) Dark Age (see p. 72).
Map ref.: TQ115905
Position: N. of Montesole Playing Fields on N. side of Uxbridge Road. It can be reached via Blythwood Road and Norman Crescent, or across the Playing Fields from the Uxbridge Road entrance. A stretch of about 260 yards of the Ditch can be seen here.

HATCH END, GRIM'S DYKE GOLF COURSE — GRIM'S DYKE (2)

See GRIM'S DYKE (1)
Map ref.: TQ135924
Position: N. side of Old Redding, along S.E. side of Golf Course. It can be seen most easily near the corner of Oxhey Lane and Old Redding when the leaves are off the hedgerows. Only a distant view can be obtained from the public footpath across the Golf Course.

SURREY
LONDON BOROUGH OF CROYDON

FARTHING DOWN

CELTIC FIELDS, SAXON BARROWS

Date: 1st century B.C. to 2nd century A.D., and 7th century A.D.
Map ref.: TQ300577
Position: ¾ mile S. of Coulsdon Station. The lynchets (field-edges) can be seen on both sides of the modern roadway to Chaldon, and an ancient field-way can be traced on its W. side. The main group of barrows is on the northern part of the Down, W. of the road; others lie farther S. at considerable intervals, also W. of the

90

road, which is on the line of an earlier track, probably of Saxon origin. The most prominent earthworks on the Down, however, are the E.—W. anti-aircraft trenches of the 1939-45 war. The lynchets and fieldway are best seen when the sun is low.

Finds made in the barrows in 1871 included a wooden cup with ornamental bands of bronze gilt, silver pins, beads, a gold circular pendant with an indented cross, buckets, a sword and iron shield-boss. The bodies were unburnt and lay with their heads to the W.

Surrey Archaeological Collections, XLII (1934), 45 ff; L (1949), 47 ff; LVI (1955), 136 ff.

LONDON BOROUGH OF MERTON

MORDEN PARK

ROUND BARROW (?)

Date: (?) Roman.
Map ref.: TQ245675
Position: In southern part of Morden Park, about 70 yards S. of cycle track and 150 yards W.S.W. of band-stand.

This large artificial mound was used in recent years as a site for a summer-house, for which purpose its top seems to have been flattened. It is unlikely that it was constructed in recent landscape gardening to provide a good view, since the site is on a promontory that has excellent views without its aid. It has therefore been recognized by the Department of the Environment as an Ancient Monument, though its date remains unknown. It is larger than most Bronze Age barrows, and it is suspected that it may be Roman. It lies only ¼ mile W. of the line of Roman Stane Street.

WIMBLEDON COMMON, (1) CAESAR'S CAMP

HILL-FORT

Date: Early Iron Age, *c.*3rd century B.C.
Map ref.: TQ223710
Position: 1¼ miles W. of Wimbledon Station, via Wimbledon Hill, entering Common opposite Marryat Road; or ¼ mile N.E. of A3, entering Common opposite Coombe Hill Road, 1 mile S. of junction with A308. The site is on the Royal Wimbledon Golf Course, and public access is limited to a path through the middle, from which only part of the circular rampart and ditch can be seen. (See fig. 24)

It has a single bank and ditch, enclosing about 12 acres, and excavation has shown that the ditch was originally 30-40 ft wide and over 12 ft deep. The bank was 30 ft broad at its base and was faced front and back with vertical timber walls. The dating is based on the evidence of pottery found in the ditch and under the bank.

The Archaeological Journal. CII (1945), 15 ff.

(2) 'QUEEN'S BUTT'

POSSIBLE LONG BARROW

Date: (?) Neolithic.
Map ref.: TQ225717
Position: On Golf Course, 600 yards N. of 'Caesar's Camp', ½ mile S.W. of windmill.

The shape of this long mound has given rise to the suggestion that it might be a long barrow, although it seems to lack the usual ditches. It was used as a firing-butt when shooting for the Queen's Prize, hence its modern name, but is not the usual shape of a firing-butt, and may have been merely adopted for this purpose. It has never been excavated. There are traces of a similar mound a little to the N.

LONDON BOROUGH OF RICHMOND UPON THAMES

RICHMOND PARK – HENRY VIII'S MOUNT

POSSIBLE BARROW

Date: (?) Bronze Age.
Map ref.: TQ185732
Position: Between Richmond Gate and Pembroke Lodge.

This mound is traditionally the spot on which Henry VIII stood to watch for the signal rocket from the Tower of London announcing Anne Boleyn's death. It was once opened and a deposit of ashes was found in the centre of it. It may well be an ancient barrow, but this is by no means certain.

E. Jesse, *Gleanings in Natural History*, 3rd series (1835) 244 f.

Museums to Visit

The London Region is comparatively poor in spectacular sites that are permanently accessible, but rich in museums where its antiquities can be seen.

The British Museum contains many of the most important finds from the region. The London Museum (Kensington Palace) has the principal collection from Greater London; Guildhall Museum the collection from the City. These two collections will shortly be united in a new Museum of London, now being built where London Wall meets Aldersgate Street.

The following museums of Greater London contain important collections of local antiquities: Cuming (Walworth Road) Gunnersbury Park, Kingston-on-Thames, Orpington, Passmore Edwards (Romford Road), Plumstead and Walthamstow. There are small collections in the following museums: Barnet, Dagenham (Valence House), Enfield (Forty Hall), Epping Forest (Chingford), Erith, Palmers Green (Broomfield) and Uxbridge (Hamson).

There are important local collections of S. Essex in the Chelmsford, Grays Thurrock and Prittlewell Priory Museums; of S.W. Hertfordshire in Hertford Museum and Verulamium Roman Museum (the latter of more than local importance); of S. Bedfordshire in Luton Museum; of S. Buckinghamshire in the County Museum at Aylesbury; of E. Berkshire in the Reading and Windsor Museums; of N. Surrey in the County Museum at Guildford; of W. Kent in the Dartford and Rochester Museums. Space does not permit mention of all the smaller museums in the outlying parts of the region that contain interesting local antiquities.

A List of Books

P. Ashby, *The Bronze Age Round Barrow in Britain,* (Phoenix, 1959).

A. Birley, *Life in Roman Britain,* (Batsford, 1964).

J. G. D. Clark, *Prehistoric England,* (Batsford, 1963).
World Prehistory—A New Outline, (C.U.P., 1969).

J. Dyer, *Discovering Regional Archaeology; Eastern England,* (Shire, 1969).

S. S. Frere (ed.), *Problems of the Iron Age in Southern Britain,* (C.B.A., 1958/9).

S. S. Frere, *Britannia, a History of Roman Britain,* (Routledge, 1967).

W. F. Grimes, *The Excavation of Roman and Mediaeval London,* (Routledge,1968).

J. Hawkes, *A Guide to the Prehistoric and Roman Monuments in England and Wales,* (Chatto and Windus, 1951).

I. D. Margary, *Roman Roads in Britain,* (John Baker, 1967).

G. W. Meates, *Lullingstone Roman Villa,* (Heinemann, 1955).
Lullingstone Roman Villa, (Small Guide; H.M.S.O., 1962).

R. Merrifield, *The Roman City of London,* (Ernest Benn, 1965).
Roman London, (Cassell, 1969).

J. N. L. Myres, *Anglo-Saxon Pottery and the Settlement of England,* (Clarendon Press, 1969).

S. Piggott, *Neolithic Cultures of the British Isles,* (C.U.P., 1954).

I. A. Richmond, *Roman Britain,* (Penguin Books, 1963).

A. L. F. Rivet (ed.), *The Roman Villa in Britain,* (Routledge, 1969).

A. L. F. Rivet, *Town and Country in Roman Britain,* (Hutchinson, 1958).

N. Thomas, *A Guide to Prehistoric England,* (Batsford, 1960).

Victoria History of the County of Middlesex, vol. I, (O.U.P., 1969).

R. E. M. Wheeler, *London and the Saxons,* (London Museum, 1935).

R. E. M. and T. V. Wheeler, *Verulamium—a Belgic and two Roman Cities,* (Society of Antiquaries, 1936).

J. Wymer, *Lower Palaeolithic Archaeology in Britain,* (Baker, 1968).

The older books may be out-of-date in interpretation, but are valuable for facts. A useful journal for the presentation of new ideas in a rapidly changing subject is the quarterly *Current Archaeology.* The principal sources for local archaeology are the journals of the County societies, namely *Transactions of the London and Middlesex Archaeological Society, Archaeologia Cantiana, Essex Archaeological Society Transactions, Hertfordshire Archaeology, Surrey Archaeological Collections,* and *Records of Buckinghamshire. The London Archaeo-* *logist* and *Kent Archaeological Review* are useful for current news. *Antiquaries Journal, Proceedings of the Prehistoric Society* and other national archaeological journals contain important papers relating to the London region.

Maps: Ordnance Survey one-inch maps. Sheets 147, 148, 159-162, 170-172. Quarter-inch map, Sheet 17. Period Maps: *Ancient Britain, South* (2nd ed., 1964), *Southern Britain in the Iron Age* (1962), *Roman Britain* (3rd ed., 1956), *Britain in the Dark Ages* (2nd ed., 1966).

Index

94

95